Selling Smoke:
Cigarette Advertising and Public Health

Kenneth E. Warner, PhD

October 1986

American Public Health Association
1015 Fifteenth Street, NW
Washington, DC 20005

The APHA Public Health Policy Series is intended to bring professional perspectives to bear on issues important to the health of the public. The views expressed are those of the authors and do not necessarily reflect the official position of the Association.

Library of Congress Cataloging-in-Publication Data

Warner, Kenneth E., 1947 -
  Selling Smoke.

  (Public health policy series)
  Bibliography: p.
  1. Tobacco—Toxicology;   2. Health education.
3. Advertising—Cigarettes.   4. Consumer education.
I.   American Public Health Association.   II. Title.   III. Series.
[DNLM: 1. Advertising.   2. Public Health.   3. Smoking.
  WA 754 W282s]
RA1242.T6W37 1986   363.1'94   86-25875
ISBN 0-87553-145-8

10/86 1 M; 6/87 1 M; 4/89 1 M

TABLE OF CONTENTS

ABOUT THE AUTHOR

The author is Professor and Chair of the Department of Public Health Policy and Administration of the University of Michigan School of Public Health. Dr. Warner was graduated from Dartmouth College and received his Ph.D. in economics from Yale University. His research has concentrated on the economics of disease prevention and health promotion, with a special emphasis on smoking and health. He has published widely on the subject and his expertise has led to memberships on the Board of Scientific Counselors of the Division of Cancer Prevention and Control, National Cancer Institute, the Research Advisory Committee of Harvard's Institute for the Study of Smoking Behavior and Policy, the American Cancer Society's Committee on Tobacco and Cancer, and the American Heart Association's Subcommittee on Smoking. Among the private and governmental organizations with which Dr. Warner consults are the Coalition on Smoking Or Health and the federal Office on Smoking and Health. He testified on tobacco policy issues before two congressional committees during the past year, including at the Oversight Hearing on Tobacco Advertising and Promotion held by the Subcommittee on Health and the Environment of the U.S. House of Representatives.

ACKNOWLEDGMENTS

My initial work on the subject of this monograph was supported by grants from the National Cancer Institute (1 R03 CA 39106-01) and the Josiah Macy, Jr., Foundation. My appreciation of the issues has benefited enormously from discussions with Virginia Ernster, John Holbrook, Eugene Lewit, Michael Pertschuk, Jesse Steinfeld, Joe Tye, and Elizabeth Whelan, all of whom have served as co-authors with me on papers on tobacco advertising and promotion. I have also derived insights from conversations with colleagues, too numerous to mention, in the fields of medicine, public health, law, advertising, and the media. Ruth Galanter, John Holbrook, and John Pinney offered detailed, helpful comments on an earlier draft. Finally, I thank Kathleen Van Wagenen for her cheerful and highly competent secretarial assistance on a very tight schedule.

ACKNOWLEDGMENT

CHAPTER 1

INTRODUCTION

According to the Surgeon General of the United States, "cigarette smoking is the chief, single, avoidable cause of death in our society and the most important public health issue of our time".[1] The source of from 270,000 to almost 500,000 fatalities every year,[2-4] smoking accounts for as many as one of every four American deaths. The cigarette is also the object of the most massive advertising and promotional campaign ever dedicated to a single product, with over $2 billion devoted to the effort in 1984.[5]

Is there a relationship between these two facts? The tobacco industry insists vehemently that cigarette promotion does not encourage use of cigarettes. Rather, they claim, promotion techniques are directed solely at, and only affect, brand shares of a market populated by confirmed smokers. By contrast, many health professionals believe that advertising is a significant determinant of young people's initiating tobacco habits and of existing smokers' continuing their habits. As such, they associate the promotion of tobacco products with the persistence of widespread smoking and its enormous disease burden.

Recently, belief in the association between advertising and tobacco use, and an independent concern with the morality of permitting tobacco promotion, have led numerous health and medical organizations to call for a ban on the promotion of tobacco products. The proposal is strong medicine, a bitter pill for the tobacco industry and the print media and a dosage of regulation that the American Civil Liberties Union has said may exceed the limits of constitutionality. At stake are such issues as freedom of commercial speech and the economic viability of scores of publications. The willingness of proponents of an ad ban to pursue their cause, in the face of the enormity of these issues, is indicative of the strength of their conviction that promoting tobacco products is wrong and represents a significant public health hazard.

With the goal of informing the ongoing debate, this monograph explores the advertising and promotion issue in some depth. Its specific objectives are to describe the nature and magnitude of promotional expenditures on cigarettes; to identify the diverse functions that advertising and promotion are alleged to serve; to

1

review the evidence on the relationship between advertising and cigarette consumption; to examine the issues involved in the ad ban proposal, as well as other policy alternatives that have received recent attention; and to offer an assessment of whether the ban should be implemented.

While many of the issues discussed in this monograph generalize across tobacco product types, most of the presentation focuses on cigarette advertising and promotion, for several reasons. One is that the debate has emerged from concern about the enormous health toll of cigarette smoking, the predominant form of tobacco use. Second, the vast majority of tobacco promotional expenditure is devoted to cigarettes, although a growing proportion is dedicated to smokeless tobacco products. Third, virtually all of the existing empirical evidence on the consequences of tobacco advertising relates to cigarettes. Given the growing use, and promotion, of smokeless tobacco, however,[6] issues and evidence presented here should be considered in the broader context of all tobacco products.

Chapters 4 through 7 constitute the heart of the monograph, addressing the objectives identified above. Chapters 2 and 3 present contextual background material, including a brief review of the demographics of smoking, an overview of the health consequences, a summary of efforts to communicate health effects to the public, an assessment of the public's current appreciation of the facts of smoking and health, and comments on associated attitudinal and behavioral change. A fundamental thesis of this monograph is that there is a logical chain connecting information flow to knowledge change, knowledge change to attitudinal change, and attitudinal change eventually to behavioral change. This logical chain applies equally to the relationship between dissemination of health information and the avoidance of smoking, and between cigarette advertising and the initiation or continuation of smoking. Chapter 3 addresses the first of these relationships, while Chapters 4 and 5 address the second.

Readers familiar with the basic facts of smoking and health can comfortably skip Chapter 2. Chapter 3 can be skimmed or omitted by readers familiar with public education and publicity on smoking's hazards and their effects on public knowledge, attitudes, and smoking behavior.

CHAPTER 2

WHO SMOKES AND TO WHAT EFFECT?

Who Smokes?

Today, the smoking population in the United States consists of roughly equal numbers of males and females, totalling about 30 percent of the adult population. The appearance of parity between males and females, however, masks important distinctions between the sexes in the age composition of smokers and in the histories of smoking by men and women. The data in Table 1, reporting smoking rates by sex over time, indicate that smoking was prevalent among men—indeed, much more prevalent than it is today—for many decades when the habit was relatively uncommon among women.

Prior to the Second World War, social taboos against smoking by women restricted the habit primarily to the male population. Arising in a major way during World War I, smoking by men rapidly grew into a habit of the majority, a phenomenon that

Table 1. Percentage of Adults Reporting Themselves to Be Smokers, U.S., by Sex and Year[a]

Year	% Males (1)	% Females (2)	% Total (3)	Ratio male to female rates (4) = (1) ÷ (2)
1935	52.5	18.1	n.a.	2.90
1955	52.6	24.5	37.6	2.15
1965	52.4	34.1	42.7	1.54
1970	44.5	31.9	37.8	1.39
1976	41.9	32.0	36.4	1.31
1980	38.3	29.4	33.6	1.30
1985	33.2	27.9	30.4	1.19

Note:
[a] For years 1965–85, the rates are for adults 20 years and older, taken from the Health Interview Survey; for 1955, adults 17 years and older, from supplement to Current Population Survey; ages not indicated for 1935.

Sources:
US Department of Health, Education, and Welfare, Public Health Service: Smoking and Health: A Report of the Surgeon General. Washington, DC: Govt. Printing Office, 1979, Table A-1; U.S. Department of Health and Human Services, PHS: The Health Consequences of Smoking for Women: A Report of the Surgeon General. Washington, DC: Govt. Printing Office,1980, Table 1; and US DHHS, PHS: Health—United States—1986. Washington, DC: Govt. Printing Office, forthcoming 1987.

persisted through the mid 1960s. Yet saying that half of men smoked understates the popularity of smoking. At the age of peak smoking prevalence, roughly from the age of 20 through the early 30s, up to 70 percent of all American men were smokers. (See Table 2.)

Table 2 also shows three critical developments in the smoking trends by the two sexes. One is the distinct decreases in smoking by men, perhaps reflected most powerfully in the fact that peak prevalence smoking reached only 40 percent of the cohort of men born 1951-60. This cohort of males appears to be the first born in the 20th century that never included a majority of smokers.

The second development is seen in the age of peak prevalence for women. Four ten-year birth cohorts of women reached peak prevalence within a five-year period, an extraordinary phenomenon reflecting the fact that smoking by women became socially acceptable only in the post-World War II era.

The third development is derivative from the first two: while men have out-numbered women in all earlier birth cohorts, the percentages of male and female smokers approached parity in the birth cohort born 1951-60. For cohorts born since then, the new smoking population has consisted of a larger proportion of females than males, a phenomenon unprecedented during this century.

The changing sex pattern of smoking among young Americans is undoubtedly the most interesting development in the epidemiology of smoking in recent years. Table 3 presents data showing

Table 2. Peak Rates of Smoking, by Sex and Birth Cohort

Birth Year	Men			Women		
	Peak Smoking Prevalence (%)	Year	Avg. Age	Peak Smoking Prevalence (%)	Year	Avg. Age
1901–10	61.9[a]	1938	32.5	23.9[a]	1958	52.5
11–20	71.3	1947	31.5	37.2	1960	44.5
21–30	69.6	1953	27.5	44.4	1958	32.5
31–40	60.8	1962	26.5	44.5	1963	27.5
41–50	58.5	1969	23.5	41.4	1970	24.5
51–60	40.3	1977	21.5	37.8	1976	20.5

Notes:
[a] Rate for 1901–10 cohort may be an underestimate, reflecting that larger proportion of ever-smokers in cohort had died at time of survey. (See Harris, JE: Cigarette smoking among successive birth cohorts of men and women in the United States during 1900–1980. JNCI 1983; 71:473–479.)

Source:
Unpublished data from J.E. Harris.

4

changes in the prevalence of regular smoking by American teen-agers. The table exhibits the clear trend through the 1970s toward higher rates of smoking among teenage girls and lower rates among teenage boys. More recent data suggest that smoking prevalence decreased among both boys and girls in the early 1980s, although the percentage of female teen smokers persisted at rates higher than those of males.[7] A focus exclusively on smoking, however, misses the rapid adoption of smokeless tobacco habits by adolescent males in recent years. With perhaps a fifth of all teenage boys being users of smokeless tobacco,[6,8,9] it is not clear that one can characterize tobacco use—as opposed to cigarette smoking—as primarily a female habit among youngsters.

Data on smoking habits reveal significant differences among groups of people defined by characteristics other than age and sex. For example, while smoking used to be associated with wealth and class, the reverse holds true in American society today. Survey results also suggest that blacks may smoke in greater numbers than whites, although probably with less intensity (i.e., fewer cigarettes per day).[3,10,11] There are also significant differences in smoking by occupation groups, with physicians the leading group of nonsmokers and blue collar workers including close to a majority as smokers.[12,13] A probable result of this shift in the demographic pattern of smoking is that the gap between the health of the affluent and poor segments of society, and between whites and blacks, seems likely to expand in the next few decades.

While there are numerous other dimensions to an exploration of smoking patterns, this brief introduction should serve to paint a portrait of the American smoker today. The essential fact is that 56 million Americans are smokers at present, including over four

Table 3. Percentages of Teenagers Reporting Themselves to Be Regular Smokers, US, by Age, Sex, and Year

Year	% Males Age (Yrs)			% Females Age (Yrs)		
	12–14	15–16	17–18	12–14	15–16	17–18
1970	5.7	19.5	37.3	3.0	14.4	22.8
1974	4.2	18.1	31.0	4.9	20.2	25.9
1979	3.2	13.5	19.3	4.3	11.8	26.2

Source:
US Department of Health, Education, and Welfare, National Institute of Education: Teenage Smoking: Immediate and Long-term Patterns. Washington, DC: Govt. Printing Office, 1979.

million teenagers. And while the prevalence of smoking has decreased significantly over the past two decades, the remaining prevalence—30 percent of the adult population—represents perhaps the most significant modifiable risk factor in our society.

Health Effects of Smoking

That cigarette smoking is hazardous to health should hardly come as a surprise. The burning cigarette has been described as a "prolific chemical factory," producing thousands of compounds, several of which are known carcinogens, while numerous others are suspected carcinogens. The gas phase of tobacco smoke includes carbon monoxide and carbon dioxide, nitrogen oxides, ammonia, at least eight volatile N-nitrosamines, hydrogen cyanide and cyanogen, close to 30 volatile sulphur compounds, more than 30 volatile nitriles, several hundred other N-containing volatile compounds, and volatile aldehydes and ketones, including formaldehyde. Turning to the particulate phase, "tar" is defined as the total particulates minus water and nicotine. The particulate phase includes nicotine and minor tobacco alkaloids, nonvolatile N-nitrosamines, aromatic amines, benzene and napthalenes, polynuclear aromatic hydrocarbons, aza-arenes, phenols, carboxylic acids, over 70 metals, including arsenic, nickel, and cadmium, pesticides, including DDT and parathion, and radioactive elements, including polonium 210 and potassium 40. The average smoker takes about a dozen puffs on roughly 30 cigarettes per day, thus inhaling the above compounds close to 400 times daily.[14]

Scientific understanding of the relationship between tobacco and a wide variety of diseases is a product primarily of the second half of the present century. However, the ill effects of smoking have been suspected for at least three and a half centuries. An illustration of that suspicion is captured in the words of King James I of England who, in 1604 in his *Counterblaste to Tobacco*, described smoking as:

> . . . a custome Lothsome to the eye, hatefull to the Nose, harmfull to the braine, dangerous to the Lungs, and in the blacke stinking fume thereof, neerest resembling the horrible Stigian smoke of the pit that is bottomeless.[15]

The very first issue of the *Journal of the American Medical Association*, published in 1883, included an anecdotal account of

6

the harmful effects of smoking by children.[16] Evidence of a more scientific nature began to emerge in the 1920s, '30s, and '40s,[17] but it was not until the late 1940s and early 1950s that major epidemiological studies were conducted and began to find their way into print. The landmark research of Wynder and Graham, published in 1950 in *JAMA*,[18] and of Doll and Hill, published in 1952 and 1954 in the *British Medical Journal*,[19,20] produced the first truly compelling evidence that lung cancer was associated with smoking. These studies opened a literature that now comprises some 50,000 research publications linking smoking to a wide variety of devastating illnesses. Collectively, this literature constitutes the single most impressive body of epidemiological and scientific knowledge associating a single risk factor with human disease.

Smoker Mortality and Morbidity

Estimates of the annual U.S. mortality toll of smoking range from 270,000[2] to close to 500,000,[4] with an estimate of 350,000 cited by the Surgeon General.[3] Among these 350,000 are 130,000 cancer deaths—approximately 30 percent of all cancer mortality—170,000 coronary heart disease deaths—again, about 30 percent of the nation's premier cause of death*—and 50,000 chronic obstructive lung disease deaths—from 80 to 90 percent of fatalities from emphysema and chronic bronchitis. If numbers such as these seem abstract, they are put into perspective by recognizing that the death toll associated with smoking is the equivalent of three fully loaded jumbo jets crashing and leaving no survivors, every single day of the year.

While it may not claim the most victims, cancer is the disease category the public most commonly associates with smoking. In part this is attributable to the fact that the earliest research on the health hazards of smoking concerned its relationship with cancer. That relationship was easier to discover because the relative risk of lung cancer—the major smoking-related cancer—is so very high. Overall, the average smoker stands a 10-fold greater chance of contracting lung cancer than someone who has never smoked, and for heavy smokers the risk rises to 15 to 25 times that of the never-smoker.[22]

---

* In a recent estimate, the Congressional Office of Technology Assessment attributed 13 percent of heart disease deaths to smoking.[21]

Lung cancer was virtually nonexistent at the turn of the century. Today, it accounts for more than a quarter of all cancer deaths. While it has long been the leading cancer killer of men, lung cancer has recently surpassed breast cancer as the leading cause of cancer death in women.[23,24] The epidemic growth of lung cancer deaths in each of men and women paralleled the growth in the prevalence of smoking two to three decades earlier. The decreasing rates of smoking among men since the mid-1960s seem to be reflected in steady and possibly falling lung cancer death rates in the 1980s.[24] While as many as 15 percent of lung cancers are diagnosed in nonsmokers, many of the nonsmoking victims of lung cancer are former smokers and others are individuals with a long history of "second-hand" exposure to tobacco smoke.

Lung cancer is not the only cancer associated with smoking. Smoking is also identified as a major cause of cancers of the oral cavity and esophagus and a contributing factor to cancers of the urinary bladder, kidney, and pancreas. All told, the 30 percent of yearly cancer deaths attributed to smoking constitute the single reason that cancer death rates have been rising in the United States. Absent smoking-related cancers, the age-adjusted cancer death rate has actually been falling.[25]

Coronary heart disease accounts for 30 percent of this country's deaths each year. While a number of uncontrollable risk factors, such as genetic predisposition, influence the CHD death rate, there are three major independent risk factors that can be modified: smoking, high blood pressure, and cholesterol. Given its prevalence and the fact that it can be avoided, smoking is commonly identified as the single most important preventable cause of CHD death. Smoking is also associated with atherosclerosis and cerebrovascular disease and is the most powerful risk factor predisposing to atherosclerotic peripheral arterial disease.[26]

Three observations highlight the importance of the relationship between smoking and heart disease. First is the assessment that the vast majority of sudden death in young adults is the result of smoking.[27] Second is the estimate that if smoking habits in this country do not change, 10 percent of Americans alive today may die from smoking-related CHD.[26] That is 24 million people. Finally, while the nation's attention has been riveted on the drama of replacing the quintessential human organ, the heart, with a mechanical substitute, few people are aware that the first three recipients of artificial hearts had collectively smoked over one million cigarettes.

While coronary heart disease has multiple important causes, chronic obstructive lung disease (COLD) does not. The vast majority of deaths due to COLD are associated with smoking and the vast majority of suffering from nonfatal emphysema and chronic bronchitis is also caused by cigarettes. Relatively few lifelong smokers escape some degree of emphysema. While many victims merely find their daily activities more difficult, others must chain themselves to mechanical breathing apparatus simply to satisfy their bodies' demands for oxygen.[1]

This last point emphasizes a second dimension of the health effects of smoking: while death is the most dramatic outcome, the most prevalent consequence of smoking is morbidity and disability. The Surgeon General estimates that more than 145 million days of excess bed disability and over 80 million days of excess work days lost are the product of smoking-related illnesses each year. Thus, while smoking is the nation's leading cause of preventable premature death, it is also the single most important source of avoidable illness and disability.[3]

The tenacity of smoking in persistently claiming its annual toll of deaths and illness is a function of the fact that the behavior is so addicting, both physically and psychologically. While the public perception is one of "habituation", tobacco dependence has all the essential characteristics of a drug dependency.[28,29] The former Director of the National Institute on Drug Abuse has labelled smoking "the most widespread form of drug dependence in our country"[30] and the American Psychiatric Association includes "tobacco use disorder" within its classification of diseases.[31] Evidence suggests that cigarettes are as difficult to kick as heroin.[29,32,33] In part this could reflect the intensity of the motivation to quit; but in part it might reflect the virtual impossibility of completely removing the agent from one's environment. Few people work in job settings that are completely devoid of smokers; one sees smokers on every city street; and, pertinent to the subject of this monograph, virtually every American is exposed daily to the attractive imagery of cigarette ads in magazines and on billboards.

Involuntary Smoking

Without question, the vast majority of the disease burden of smoking is imposed by smokers on themselves. Nevertheless, a great deal of contemporary attention focuses on the effects of

9

"smokers' pollution" on the nonsmoking majority of the population. Long recognized as a significant annoyance and source of physical irritation, tobacco smoke in the environment has been indicted as a hazard to the health of nonsmokers. While smoke released into the atmosphere is rapidly diffused, in certain settings smoking leaves markedly elevated levels of carbon monoxide and other products of combustion. These settings include bars and restaurants, workplaces populated by significant numbers of smokers, and the homes of heavy smokers. Nonsmokers, including infants, heavily exposed to tobacco smoke have nicotine levels in their blood and urine that would be produced by smoking one or two cigarettes per day.[34,35] Further, the lung function of nonsmoking workers employed in a smoky setting has been measured as comparable to that of light smokers.[36]

Given the toxicity of tobacco smoke in smokers, and the carcinogenicity of constituents of smoke demonstrated in the laboratory, it is readily comprehensible that laypersons and scientists alike would be concerned about the possible hazards that environmental tobacco smoke poses for nonsmokers. As a result, the health effects of involuntary smoking have become a topic of substantial scientific interest. A growing body of literature—one bibliography listed 800 publications as of the end of 1985[37]— implicates smoking as a risk factor in conditions arising in nonsmokers from cradle (literally, before the cradle) to grave.

Reflecting the fear that cancer evokes, the greatest public concern has concentrated on reports that long-term involuntary smoking may double the risk of lung cancer. In 1981, a study published by Hirayama in the *British Medical Journal* found a two-fold increase in this risk in the nonsmoking wives of smoking husbands in Japan.[38] This study received a great deal of attention in both the scientific and lay public communities, the latter in part because the Tobacco Institute, the industry's Washington lobby, attempted to discredit the study and publicized its interpretation of the research. In full-page ads in major newspapers and magazines,[39] the Institute emphasized scientific criticism of the work and cited an American Cancer Society study that failed to find evidence of involuntary smoking-induced lung cancer.[40] Since 1980, close to 20 studies have been published on the relationship between involuntary smoking and lung cancer, the majority finding a statistically significantly elevated risk for people exposed over many years to large doses of involuntary smoke.[41]

A doubling or trebling of risk for an individual exposed to a risk factor represents a substantial percentage increase in risk, but the likelihood of experiencing the disease in question is also a function of the underlying prevalence of the condition. In the case of lung cancer, the likelihood that a lifelong nonsmoker will contract lung cancer is so small that a doubling of that risk remains relatively small. Thus the literature on involuntary smoking lung cancer should not be misinterpreted as suggesting that the nonsmoking spouse of a smoker is likely to get cancer as the result of his or her spouse's tobacco habit.

At the same time, the widespread prevalence of involuntary smoke-exposed people suggests that a substantial number of cases may be found in the aggregate. Repace and Lowrey have estimated that involuntary smoking causes between 500 and 5000 cases of lung cancer each year throughout the United States.[42] While these numbers pale in comparison with the total number of lung cancer deaths—126,000 in 1985[23]—even the lower end of the range would make environmental tobacco smoke the single most important cancer-causing pollutant to which the general public is exposed. And a doubling of cancer risk associated with any other environmental hazard is commonly deemed a strong basis for regulatory action.

While public anxiety focuses on cancer, better established consequences of involuntary smoking receive relatively less attention. Prominent among these are the effects of tobacco smoke on the fetus. Reliant on its mother's blood supply, the developing fetus is perhaps the preeminent "involuntary smoker" in society. A substantial body of research has established that maternal smoking is a major risk factor in low birthweight, itself associated with a number of hazards, and in spontaneous abortion, fetal death, and neonatal death.[43] The risk posed by smoking mothers to their unborn babies has led biomedical scientists recently to coin the descriptor, fetal tobacco syndrome.[44]

The risks associated with parental smoking both precede and follow pregnancy. Research suggests that smoking is a factor in impotence and that, short of impotence, it reduces the probability that a couple will be able to conceive.[45,46] Following birth, the children of smokers face a long list of ailments their contemporaries with nonsmoking parents experience with lesser frequency. The child of a mother who smoked during pregnancy faces an elevated risk of developmental disabilities, both physical (e.g., height) and

11

mental. The children of smokers experience an increased number of respiratory illnesses, a relationship that shows a clear dose-response effect: children having two smoking parents experience more respiratory illness than children having one smoking parent; the latter, in turn, have more illness than children of nonsmoking parents.[47,48]

While the victim of fetal tobacco syndrome is as innocent as can be, there is a second class of individuals for whom a compelling case can be made that they are truly the ultimate innocent victims of other people's smoking. These are the children who are burned while they sleep because a neighbor or parent failed to extinguish a cigarette. Cigarettes are the cause of an estimated 30 to 40 percent of home fires. Some 2300 Americans die each year in cigarette-ignited fires and another 5000 are burned.[49] The irony is that few of these injuries and deaths would occur if the cigarette manufacturers did not treat their papers and tobaccos with chemical additives designed to keep cigarettes burning essentially continuously. Absent the additives, the cigarettes would self-extinguish when not puffed upon, thereby substantially reducing or eliminating the risk of igniting a fire. The manufacturers insist, however, that a "fire-safe" cigarette is not technologically feasible, or at least that self-extinguishing cigarettes would be unacceptable to smokers. The issue is being examined at present by a congressionally mandated committee including representatives from both the health community and the tobacco industry.

Composition of the Cigarette

The concern about manufacturing cigarettes to burn continuously illustrates a broader phenomenon: the composition of the cigarette has changed markedly over the past three and a half decades, and the changes have numerous health implications, some obvious and some quite subtle and even unexpected.

The cigarette of the 1940s consisted primarily of shredded tobacco leaf, often including some sweetened leaf, wrapped in largely unadulterated cigarette paper. Today's product, by contrast, contains much less tobacco, which has been "puffed" so that a given weight fills a greater volume, the tobacco includes processed stems and other parts of the plant, the tobacco and cigarette papers are treated with hundreds of additives to enhance flavor and improve

12

burning, and the cigarette is commonly tipped with a filter, itself an intricate product comprised of a wide variety of substances.*

At first blush, the concept of the low tar and nicotine (t/n) cigarette appears attractive. To the extent that it reduces the smoker's ingestion of tars, nicotine, carbon monoxide, and the other constituents of tobacco smoke, it should reduce health risks. Furthermore, for the confirmed smoker who cannot or will not quit, the low t/n product might offer an alternative that would reduce risk without eliminating the habit.

The perception than low t/n smoking is "safe," or at least safer, is widespread, as we see in the next chapter. This perception accounted for the rapid diffusion of low t/n cigarettes through the decade of the 1970s. As Figure 1 indicates, low t/n cigarettes (defined as 15 mg or less tar per cigarette, as measured by the Federal Trade Commission) constituted an insignificant component of the market in the late 1960s and early 1970s. From the mid-1970s through 1981, however, the low t/n share of the market rose from 10 to 15 percent to 60 percent. Since then, the low t/n share

---

* One of the earliest filters, marketed with the theme that it reduced the smoker's exposure to potentially hazardous substances in cigarette smoke, was the Kent Micronite filter. The Micronite filter was made of asbestos.[50,51]

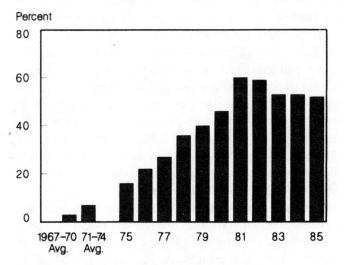

Figure 1. Low-Tar Share of Cigarette Market

Source:
US Department of Agriculture, Economic Research Service: Tobacco Outlook and Situation Report. TS-194 (March 1986). Washington, DC: Govt. Printing Office, 1986, p. 6.

has backed off, but the low t/n cigarette has remained the dominant product on the market.

Evidence on the health impacts of low t/n smoking is limited, in large part reflecting the relative novelty of the product. In part, too, demographic differences in smokers between the regular smoker in the first half of the century and the low t/n smoker of the 1980s make assessment of the differential effects of low t/n cigarettes a still more complex endeavor.

Despite these problems, there is some evidence that suggests that low t/n smokers have a lower risk of smoking-related cancer than do smokers of regular cigarettes, assuming that the number of cigarettes smoked does not increase, although the low t/n smoker's cancer risk remains substantially above that of the nonsmoker.[52] There is no evidence, however, that low t/n cigarettes significantly reduce other smoking-related risks, such as heart disease.

Little is known about the health effects of the hundreds of additives that are found in the modern cigarette. While several of the identified additives are known or suspected carcinogens, virtually all are present in minute or trace amounts. Still, the frequency with which the average smoker puffs on cigarettes means that exposure might not be inconsequential.

The picture of the low t/n cigarette as a "safer" cigarette is much more deceptive than it appears at first. There are several reasons to suspect that low t/n cigarettes may have *increased* the risks of smoking for many people and failed to reduce them for others. The existence of low t/n cigarettes may account for a larger population of smokers than would exist had the regular medium- and high-tar products remained the only options on the market. Many potential quitters may have decided to adopt low-tar ciga-rettes as an alternative to quitting. In addition, the epidemic of smoking among girls and young women may be explained in part by the availability of the less harsh low-tar products, a cigarette that makes initiation of smoking habits easier.[53]

Low t/n cigarettes may have failed to reduce risks for confirmed smokers who "switch down" to the low-tar product because, consciously or otherwise, many smokers compensate for the reduced yields of the low t/n products. As smoking is addictive, and nicotine is the addicting substance, the lesser yields of the low t/n products force smokers to find ways to "make up" for the reduced drug yield. Among the more obvious ways are smoking more cigarettes, inhaling deeper on individual cigarettes, puffing more frequently, and smoking further down the cigarette. The first of these may be a major factor in explaining the increase that has been observed in the average daily cigarette consumption of smokers.

A less obvious means of compensating for the reduced nicotine yield of the modern cigarette is the often unconscious subversion of filtration systems that account for much of the reduction in yield. A common technological approach to reducing yields involves placing a ring of tiny perforations midway down the filter. The function of the perforations is to allow air to be pulled into the cigarette when the smoker draws on the cigarette. The air mixes with the smoke and thereby dilutes it, reducing the yield of tar and nicotine. In some brands of cigarettes, these perforations are readily visible; in others, they cannot be seen by the naked eye.

Whenever a smoker occludes some of these holes, less air is drawn into the cylinder and hence more smoke is inhaled. Some smokers intentionally subvert the filtration system, either by placing tape around the holes or by snapping off the filters, apparently in the belief that the low yields of tar and nicotine are inherent in the tobacco itself, with the filter and its perforations simply being a nuisance. Occlusion also takes place quite naturally and unconsciously when smokers hold cigarettes between their fingers at the location of the perforations, or when their lips block the holes while puffing on the cigarettes. Blocking the perforations, partially or completely, raises the effective yield of tars, nicotine, carbon monoxide, and other components of smoke from 50 to 300 percent, thereby converting the rated low t/n cigarette into a medium or high t/n cigarette.[54]

The evidence for nicotine regulation is abundant and varied in nature. For many years, Schachter and his colleagues have investigated the circumstances in which smokers increase their consumption of cigarettes, relating consumption changes to social situations and accompanying changes in body chemistry. They have found, for example, that increases in cigarette consumption while smokers are at parties or are under stress are associated with acidification of the urine. When stress and urinary pH were manipulated independently in one experiment, they found that smoking correlated more closely with urinary pH than with stress. This supported their hypothesis that heavy smokers smoke for nicotine, rather than social reasons.[55]

More recently, a number of studies have documented that blood and urine levels of smoke products do not vary substantially according to the tar and nicotine ratings of smokers' cigarettes. In 1980 Russell and his colleagues reported that differences in rated nicotine yields could explain only four percent of the variation in blood nicotine concentrations.[56] In reinterpreting Russell's data, Kozlowski *et al.* found that the impact of the rated delivery was statistically significant and more substantial than Russell had indicated, but that the impact remained far short of the differences in rated yields.[57] More recently, several other studies have also found little variation in blood and urine concentrations compared with variations in brand delivery ratings.[58,59] Together, these studies constitute powerful biochemical evidence that smokers do find ways to "make up" for the technology of reducing a cigarette's nicotine delivery.

The Other Side of the Smoking and Health "Controversy"

As noted above, the evidence implicating smoking in the deaths of millions of Americans represents the most substantial and well-documented epidemiological case ever developed concerning any human behavior hazardous to health. Nevertheless, the tobacco industry continues to insist that the evidence against smoking is merely circumstantial. While the industry's case has little scientific merit, its presentation to the public is an essential ingredient in consideration of the roles and impacts of promotion of cigarettes. Ever since the first scientific evidence began to emerge, the industry has employed a promotional strategy designed to reassure smokers that the health issue was unresolved, or to downplay smokers' perception of the severity of the risks associated with smoking. The very notion of using words like "other side" and "controversy" illustrates how the language employed has been intended to connote a balance in the evidence pro and con risk. As we shall see in the next chapter, survey studies probing the depth of the public's appreciation of the hazards of tobacco suggest that the industry may have been successful in defusing the perception of risk.

At the heart of the industry's side of the story is the constitutional argument, the notion that people who choose to smoke are different from people who do not and that the former are more susceptible to the diseases associated with smoking, but for constitutional reasons other than smoking. The constitutional hypothesis is not disturbed by the fact that people who quit smoking experience a reduction in tobacco-related disease risks, with risks falling the longer the quitter remains abstinent. The explanation offered here is that quitters are constitutionally more like never-smokers, and presumably long-term quitters are still more like never-smokers.[60-62] Obviously, this argument is perfectly circular. Scientists have presented ample evidence to refute the hypothesis, including twin studies in monkeys,[3] but the industry and the handful of scientists who adhere to the hypothesis can always appeal to that circularity.

The industry does not deny the statistical relationship between smoking and a wide variety of diseases. Rather, it labels this evidence "correlation" and not "causation". The industry's appeal to this distinction has long been a source of aggravation to scientists because, while it has an element of truth—*by definition*, statistics can never prove causation—the terminological distinction can be abused in appealing to a statistically unsophisticated public. Epidemiologists have defined logical conditions which should lead an unbiased party to interpret correlations as causation, and rarely have these conditions been as well met as in the case of smoking and disease. The conditions are:

1. the consistency of the association
2. the strength of the association
3. the specificity of the association
4. the temporal relationship of the association
5. the coherence of the association[63]

In addition to the rigor of the epidemiological evidence, there is laboratory animal evidence in which, for example, the tars in cigarette smoke have induced cancers on the skin of mice and smoking itself has produced lung cancer in dogs.

What kind of evidence would the tobacco industry accept to resolve the scientific "controversy"? Presumably they would have difficulty denying the findings of a major, multi-decade, controlled trial in which scientists randomly selected a control group of people who would never be permitted to use tobacco products throughout their lives, and an experimental group who would be required to become and remain regular smokers. Short of this approach, which has rather obvious practical and ethical limitations, it is difficult to conceive of any evidence against smoking that would satisfy proponents of the constitutional hypothesis. Yet while the industry seems to insist on an unobtainable level of evidence to find smoking a cause of disease, they indiscriminately publicize scientific studies that question the smoking-disease connection, irrespective of the quality of the studies.

The industry has a clear need to persist in portraying the case against smoking as unproven. It has a legal need: an admission that smoking was hazardous, and that the industry has long known this, would be tantamount to a plea of guilty in the dozens of product liability lawsuits now filed against the industry, with a virtually inexhaustible supply of lawsuits sure to follow such an admission. Furthermore, and perhaps equally fundamentally, the industry would no longer be able to engage in the charade of portraying smoking to its customers as a pleasurable and innocent habit.

In recent years, the R.J. Reynolds Company has attempted to sway public opinion with a series of advertisements that it inaugurated under the banner of wanting to have "an open debate." As leaders of all the major voluntary associations were quick to point out, there is nothing to debate in the health arena, and Reynolds was the only "side" of the "debate" to have the resources to present its case to the reading public in full-page advertisements in prominent newspapers and magazines.

The Reynolds ads have addressed a wide variety of subjects, ranging from the undesirability of legislating restrictions on smoking in public places, to the Company's assurance that it does not want children to smoke,* to the undesirability of smoking in bed.

But one ad has had an explicit health theme and has captured the attention of the health and regulatory communities. Entitled "Of Cigarettes and Science," the text misinterpreted the findings of a major national study to suggest that cigarette smoking may not cause heart disease.[64] The American Heart Association and other health organizations believed that the misinterpretation was willful, with the intent of misleading—and reassuring—the smoking

---

* Many health professionals have found this particular theme to be the most repugnant, simply because it cannot possibly be true. The vast majority of smokers—an estimated 90 percent—start smoking as teenagers and pre-teens and become addicted. The reality is that the industry needs to have over two million children start smoking each year—well over 5000 per day—simply to replace the adult smokers who die or quit smoking, in order to keep the aggregate number of smokers from falling.

public, and perhaps potential smokers as well. The matter was brought to the Federal Trade Commission to investigate whether remedial action was warranted under the Commission's responsibility to assure that advertising is neither false nor misleading. On June 16, 1986, concluding that the ad did misrepresent the facts and misled the public, the Commission issued an administrative complaint against the company.[65] Less than two months later, an administrative law court judge ruled against the Commission.

Another example of the industry's unbalanced quest for "balance" in the "debate" on the hazards of tobacco occurred in 1984 when R.J. Reynolds purchased full-page advertising space in major publications to counter concern accorded the risks of second-hand smoke.[66] Among the arguments the company presented in the text was the fact that one of "the tobacco industry's biggest critics," Lawrence Garfinkel of the American Cancer Society, had not found any evidence of involuntary smoking-induced lung cancer in an ACS study.[40] Garfinkel claims that his finding was taken out of context.[67] In a recent case-control study designed to examine the involuntary smoking issue, Garfinkel and his colleagues did find a statistically significant risk of lung cancer associated with involuntary smoking.[68] In this case, however, Reynolds chose not to publicize the findings.

The tobacco industry's public presentations regarding smoking and health date back into the early decades of the century. In less constrained and less sophisticated days, the image of smoking as a nonhazardous behavior was promoted explicitly in cigarette ads. Beginning more than half a century ago, the manufacturers of Lucky Strikes assured readers of their ads that Luckies caused "No throat irritation - no cough." "Do you inhale?" readers were asked, "What's there to be afraid of?" R.J. Reynolds claimed that Camel cigarettes steadied the nerves, provided "a harmless restoration of the flow of natural body energy," aided digestion, and increased manual dexterity. The producers even evoked the public's image of the health-conscious medical profession to sell cigarettes. American Brands told ad readers that "20,679 physicians say Luckies are less irritating to your throat." R.J. Reynolds responded that "More doctors smoke Camel than any other brand." L&M cigarettes were presented as "just what the doctor ordered," while Philip Morris cigarettes were "recognized by eminent medical authorities."[69]

About three decades ago, the presidents of major cigarette

manufacturers and warehousers and growers associations issued a public assurance of their concern to sell the public a safe product, to engage in research, and to share with the public what they knew about the risks of smoking. They also stated that "We accept an interest in people's health as a basic responsibility, paramount to every other consideration in our business . . . We always have and always will cooperate closely with those whose task it is to safeguard the public health."[70] In 1986 the president of R.J. Reynolds, Gerald Long, told a magazine interviewer, "If I saw or thought there were any evidence whatsoever that conclusively proved that, in some way, tobacco was harmful to people, and I believed it in my heart and my soul, then I would get out of the business and I wouldn't be involved in it."[71]

CHAPTER 3

PUBLICITY AND EDUCATION ON THE HAZARDS OF SMOKING: NATURE AND EFFECTS

Publicity and Public Education

The very fact that the tobacco industry has found it necessary to try to counter the image of smoking as dangerous suggests that that image has been conveyed to the public. The financial resources available to transmit the health message pale in comparison with those used by the industry to obscure the message and promote their product. Nevertheless, there are numerous and varied methods that have been used to communicate the hazards. This section indicates the principal sources of information and considers associated changes in the nation's smoking habits. The following section considers how effectively the public has heard and understood that information. A third section briefly identifies implications.

Media Communication of Scientific Findings

The heart of the antismoking campaign,* and its essential motivation, has always been the body of scientific research that has identified and elucidated the links between smoking and disease. By itself, however, the scientific literature is much like a new automobile without any gas: it may be well-designed, interesting, and attractive, but it isn't going to go anywhere, and the only people who will be able to appreciate it are those who work on the assembly line. The gasoline fueling the smoking-and-health engine has always been the news media. It is newspapers, magazines, radio, and television that have picked up on scientific

---

* "Antismoking campaign" is used as a summary descriptor for the largely uncoordinated activities of a variety of voluntary organizations and public and private sector agencies united only by their objective of reducing the toll of smoking. These activities are as diverse as antismoking public service announcements and the marketing of aids to cessation. We examine primarily the "information arm" of the campaign, efforts to communicate the hazards of smoking to the public.

findings about smoking, translated them into layman's English, and transmitted them to the reading, listening, and viewing public.

The first significant discussion of the hazards of smoking by the media occurred in the early 1950s, most notably in the *Reader's Digest*. As indicated above, the first major research linking smoking to lung cancer was performed in the late 1940s and published in the early 1950s. With such forbidding titles as "Tobacco Smoking as a Possible Etiologic Factor in Bronchiogenic Carcinoma"[18] and medical journals as publication vehicles, the early findings might have remained epidemiological esoterica had *Reader's Digest* not distilled their essence and produced articles with such provocative titles as "Cancer by the Carton."[72] This article and others in the *Digest*[73,74] grabbed the public's attention and contributed to a public reaction that was swift and dramatic. In 1953 and 1954, adult per capita cigarette consumption—total national cigarette consumption divided by the number of adults over age 17—fell two years in a row for the first time in the century. As Figure 2 indicates, previous

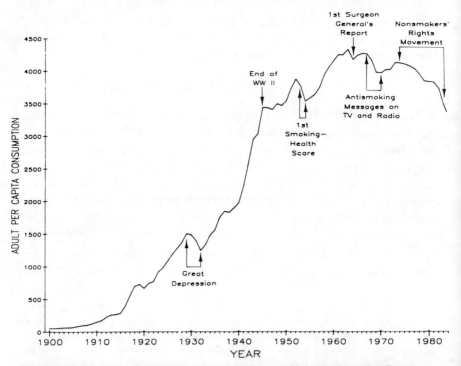

Figure 2. Adult per Capita Cigarette Consumption and Major Antismoking Events
Source:
Warner KE: Cigarette advertising and media coverage of smoking and health. New Engl J Med 1985; 312: 387.

Table 4. Filter-Tip Share of Cigarette Market

Year	% Filters	Year	% Filters
1949	0.3	1968	74.9
1950	0.6	1969	77.5
1951	0.7	1970	80.1
1952	1.3	1971	82.4
1953	2.9	1972	83.7
1954	9.2	1973	85.4
1955	18.7	1974	86.7
1956	27.6	1975	87.7
1957	38.0	1976	88.5
1958	45.3	1977	89.4
1959	48.7	1978	90.9
1960	50.9	1979	91.8
1961	52.5	1980	92.5
1962	54.6	1981	92.7
1963	58.0	1982	93.2
1964	60.9	1983	93.6
1965	64.4	1984	94.2
1966	68.2	1985	94.6
1967	72.4		

Source:
US Department of Agriculture, Economic Research Service: Tobacco Outlook and Situation Report. Washington, DC: Govt. Printing Office, various issues.

decreases in per capita consumption were rare events and lasted only a year. Their causes were the economic disruption of the Great Depression and the end of World War II.*

While per capita consumption fell, the market share of filter-tipped cigarettes soared. Virtually unknown in the late 1940s and very early 1950s, filters were an innovation intended to blunt health concerns. Advertisements heralded the filters' abilities to capture undesirable elements in the smoke. As is seen in Table 4, the apparent impact of the *Reader's Digest* and other lay press articles was swift and substantial. The market share of filter-tipped cigarettes jumped from 1.3 percent in 1952 to 2.9 percent in 1953, the first year of serious public coverage of the lung cancer link, to 9.2 percent the following year, and to 18.7 percent a year later. By

---

* Cigarettes were distributed free to soldiers during the War. In addition to being smoked by the GIs, they were used for bartering for other goods and services. The return home of the soldiers altered two conditions that had caused cigarette consumption to rise sharply during the War: cigarettes were no longer free to large numbers of Americans and their value as a barter commodity had evaporated.

1960—only seven years after the first public coverage—half of all cigarettes purchased in the United States were filter-tipped. The filter-tipped share of the market rose steadily thereafter, reaching 90 percent in 1978.*

Beginning in the mid-1950s, coverage of the hazards of smoking became less prominent and the seemingly inexorable climb in per capita consumption resumed. Despite continuing accumulation of damning evidence by the scientific community, per capita consumption rapidly returned to its pre-1953 trend line and continued to grow annually through 1963. (See Figure 2.)

1964 was a seminal year in the history of smoking and health. Two years after being appointed to advise the Surgeon General, a neutral expert panel** issued what has come to be known as the first Surgeon General's report on smoking and health, a thoroughly documented review of the evidence that concluded that the link between smoking and lung cancer in men was strong enough to be labeled causal and that associations with other chronic illnesses warranted consideration as serious risk factors.[75]

Publication of the Surgeon General's report was a landmark event that received ample press coverage. Again, as a decade earlier, the coverage seems to be responsible for a drop that year in per capita consumption—a 3.5 percent decrease that was a statistically significant fall from the upward sloping trend line.[76] This was only the second decrease in per capita consumption in the post-War period and both occurred during years of substantial media publicity on the hazards of smoking.

An idiosyncratic episode, occurring more than a decade later, further illustrates the power of the media, covering science, to influence behavior. In 1978, an official of the National Cancer Institute, Gio Gori, and a colleague, C.J. Lynch, wrote a paper suggesting that smokers of the very lowest tar and nicotine cigarettes might not be subjecting themselves to an identifiable increased risk of disease.[77] The media jumped on the story, in

---

* A nonhealth explanation for the rapid growth in filter-tipped cigarettes is that women, who were just entering the smoking market in large numbers after World War II, preferred the new product because it was neater and less dirty than the standard unfiltered cigarette. While this may have contributed to the appeal of filter-tipped cigarettes, most experts believe that the health scare of the early 1950s was the most important factor.

** Its membership included scientists who were then smokers. All of the panel's members were approved by the tobacco industry.

many instances interpreting it as evidence that low t/n smoking was "safe" smoking. For several weeks thereafter, sales of Carlton cigarettes, the lowest rated t/n cigarette on the market, soared.

The scientists' analysis was flawed in numerous ways, however, having been based on an untenable premise. The article received ample criticism in the *Journal of the American Medical Association* in which it had been published.[78,79] The criticisms and corrections suggested that the findings were unwarranted due to the flaws inherent in the analysis. Subsequent research has demonstrated convincingly that the premise of the Gori-Lynch study was unjustified. Yet neither the immediate criticisms of the article nor these subsequent studies have received more than a small fraction of the attention devoted to the dramatic, if erroneous, Gori-Lynch article. Today, despite scores of scientific statements to the contrary, a sizable minority of Americans continues to believe that smoking low t/n cigarettes is either not harmful to health or else not very harmful.[80]

Scientific findings are not the only smoking-and-health news that the media has transmitted to the public. Much of what has received attention since the first Surgeon General's report relates to public policy on smoking and health, itself the product of the scientific understanding that began to develop in the 1940s.

The emergence of public policy interest in smoking and health dates from the mid-1960s, spawned by the findings reported in the Surgeon General's report. Indeed, while scientists continued to probe the connections between smoking and illness, publication of the Surgeon General's report moved the center of attention on the smoking issue from the scientist's laboratory to the public forum. Congress debated the issue and federal agencies became involved, most notably including the Federal Trade Commission. State legislatures also began to consider public policies related to smoking. State excise taxes were raised at an unprecedented clip[81] and the FTC initiated its advertising restriction and labeling requirements. Yet per capita cigarette consumption headed upwards again in 1965 and 1966, once the widespread media coverage of 1964 had dissipated.

In 1967, a young attorney named John Banzhaf won a remarkable legal victory by convincing the Federal Communications Commission that smoking was a controversial issue and, as such, that broadcast advertising of cigarettes was subject to the Commission's Fairness Doctrine. The Fairness Doctrine required that broadcasters provide balanced coverage of controversial issues, and hence, when necessary, that they donate air time to ensure balance. This episode created one of the most fascinating chapters in the history of smoking and health, the only period during which the antismoking message was delivered to the public frequently in an advertising format. Television and radio stations were required to donate air time to the antismoking message to balance the pro-smoking message conveyed by cigarette ads. At the beginning of the period, many of the stations interpreted "balance" as requiring no more than a minute of antismoking message for every 12 minutes of paid smoking advertisements, with the former concentrated outside of prime time. But following Banzhaf's monitoring of the situation and reporting his findings to the FCC, actions against major New York stations led to an improved ratio nationwide.[82]

At its peak, the antismoking message received about one minute for every three minutes of smoking ads, again with the latter receiving the best air time. But the effects of the health messages seem to have been substantial. In 1967 per capita consumption turned down and it continued to decrease each of the years of the Fairness Doctrine period—1967-1970. This was the first four-year decrease in per capita consumption to ever occur. Its coinciding perfectly with the Fairness Doctrine years, and its cessation the year that cigarette ads were removed from the airwaves (which negated the legal need for the Fairness Doctrine antismoking messages), constitute substantial circumstantial evidence that the antismoking publicity had a significant deterrence function.

This circumstantial evidence has been supported by statistical studies that found that the antismoking messages were more effective in discouraging smoking than the pro-smoking ads were in encouraging it.[83] Further evidence that the antismoking publicity had an impact is the observation that people increased their underreporting of their smoking by a significant amount between 1966, the year preceding the Fairness Doctrine messages, and 1970, the final year of the messages. During that period, total national cigarette consumption fell by one percent (an impressive figure, since the smoking-age population was increasing by 6.6 percent); but on surveys, people's reporting of their cigarette consumption fell by almost 9.5 percent. The increase in underreporting is consistent with the observation that people tend to underreport activities that imply a personal threat or a social stigma, and that the Fairness Doctrine ads increased both the perception of personal threat and social impropriety.[84]

With the possible exception of the publicity accorded former HEW Secretary Califano's announcement of a new antismoking campaign in 1978, since 1970 there has been no single smoking-and-health event that is comparable in its uniqueness and visibility to those reviewed above. At the same time, there have been many events that have warranted the attention of the media and hence the public. These range from the annual publication of Surgeon General's reports to congressional attempts to reduce the tobacco subsidy, introduce stronger rotating health warnings on cigarette packs and ads, and increase and then maintain the federal excise tax on cigarettes; to the American Medical Association's call for a ban on promotion of tobacco products.

Perhaps the most striking smoking-and-health phenomenon of the 1970s and 1980s has been the passage of nonsmokers' rights legislation (clean indoor air laws) in dozens of states and municipalities. In the 1970s, the locus of activity was at the state level.[81] In the early 1980s, the locus shifted to the local level, and by the mid-1980s a further if subtle shift was visible in the activation of businesses themselves as agents of introducing environmental protection for the nonsmoker.[85] The importance of the nonsmokers' rights movement, in the context of the present study, is that, like many of its public policy predecessors, it has generated a substantial amount of media attention. While most of that attention has concentrated at the jurisdictional level at which legislation is being contemplated (i.e., the state or locality), a few of the battles for clean indoor air laws have achieved national prominence. In particular, the unsuccessful efforts of Californians to achieve a state clean indoor air law received national press attention, in part due to the aggressive and well-funded opposition provided by the Tobacco Institute and the cigarette companies. San Franciscans' adoption of a strong smoking restriction law in 1983 also received national attention. The latter was the first ballot initiative that succeeded against the tobacco industry's heavily funded war chest: reports from the San Francisco campaign indicate that the industry spent $1.2 million, several dollars for every eligible voter, in its efforts to defeat the initiative.[86]

Through the 1970s, decreases in per capita cigarette consumption, which have occurred every single year since 1973 (see Figure 2), paralleled increases in the activities and success of the nonsmokers' rights movement.[87] The movement has helped to keep the smoking issue in the press and hence in the minds of the public.

Crediting the media with having educated the public about the basic facts of smoking and health is not the same as saying that the media have done an adequate job of covering the tobacco and health story. To the contrary, a substantial body of evidence indicts the media for having evaded the subject, primarily as the result of the media's dependence on cigarette advertising revenue. This evasion, it has been suggested, is responsible in part for the public's surprisingly shallow understanding of the hazards of tobacco, examined later in this chapter. That limited understanding, it appears, contributes to the maintenance of smoking habits by thousands and perhaps millions of Americans who might have quit smoking, or never started in the first place, if they had been adequately informed about the dangers of smoking. The role of the media in this context constitutes one of the principal emphases of Chapter 5's consideration of the impact of tobacco advertising.

Public Policy Not Related to the Media

While much of the educational value of governmental policy on smoking and health has derived from media coverage, several public policies have been debated, adopted, and implemented, and have educated the public, without relying on media coverage. These have ranged from school health education on tobacco to package labeling requirements to excise taxation. Clearly the most direct non-media educational policy has been school health education on tobacco. This effort is central to any antismoking campaign; we devote an independent discussion to it below.

Among other policies, ostensibly the most directly education-oriented has been the congressional requirement that cigarette packages and ads bear the Surgeon General's health warning. Initially adopted in 1965, the warning labeling requirement has been modified twice, most recently in 1985 when four rotating labels were introduced. A similar labeling requirement was extended to smokeless tobacco products by congressional action the same year. While the labeling of cigarette ads achieves its educational value through the media—i.e., from readers' seeing the warnings in print media and billboard ads—the direct labeling of individual packages can only educate by the purchaser's, or potential purchaser's, reading the package itself.

A 1981 Federal Trade Commission study called the labels ineffective, noting that most smokers were essentially oblivious to the warning, familiarity having bred an almost unanimous ability to "tune it out."[80] Whether the new more specific rotating labels will achieve any appreciable increase in capturing smokers' attention remains to be seen. All told, the evidence suggests that the warning label may have outlived its usefulness as a significant educational tool, at least in its current format.* Nevertheless, its value in emphasizing the basic danger of smoking in its early years may have been considerable.

Other public policies are not self-consciously concerned with informing the public, yet ironically some of them may have substantially more "educational value" than explicit education policies. Foremost among these is an increase in cigarette excise taxes, at the federal, state, or municipal level. While it seems likely that taxes have been increased primarily to raise revenue,[81] the smoking and health consequences of taxation have been an increasingly visible component of legislative debates on proposed tax increases.[88] Indirectly, taxes serve an educational function by conveying to tobacco users that their habits are expensive. Whether many users interpret the expense in health and social terms is problematic; yet it seems likely that the singling out of tobacco products serves a reinforcing function in educating users and potential users that tobacco consumption is a costly behavior, in more than just monetary terms. Raising taxes has been demonstrated to have a substantial smoking deterrence effect.[89,90]

A similar interpretation can be accorded clean indoor air laws. While much of their educational impact is achieved through media coverage, both their physical manifestations—the profusion of no smoking signs, for example—and their subtle impact on the social milieu seem likely to serve a public educational function.

The Voluntary Agencies

The nation's major health voluntary agencies, the American Cancer Society, American Heart Association, and American Lung

---

* The FTC study proposed that the format be changed to draw attention to the new messages, for example by encapsulating the message in a circle with a large arrow, instead of the familiar plain white rectangular box.[80]

Association, have played significant roles in disseminating information on the hazards of tobacco. This has been achieved by a wide variety of interventions, ranging from development, testing, and distribution of educational materials for the schools, to production and dissemination of counteradvertising, posters or radio or television spots—public service announcements (PSAs)—that carry an antismoking message, often parodying pro-smoking advertisement imagery.

The antismoking advertising and educational activities of the voluntaries are no match for the resources of the tobacco industry. To put the matter into perspective, the sum total of the budgets of the three major agencies is in the vicinity of half a billion dollars per year. If 10 percent of this amount were devoted to production and distribution of materials and programs, and purchase of advertising space, the resource base for such activities over the course of an entire year would amount to only the equivalent of nine days' worth of tobacco industry expenditures dedicated to promotion of cigarettes. When one recognizes that each of the voluntaries has many important concerns other than smoking, the limited ability of the agencies to educate the public becomes clear.

The heyday of the voluntaries' communicating the hazards of tobacco to the public was the Fairness Doctrine era. At its peak, the donated television and radio time constituted a subsidy of approximately $200 million (in 1985 dollars) to the antismoking cause. The effectiveness of the Fairness Doctrine messages seems all the more remarkable when one considers how relatively amateurish the early counteradvertising efforts were. The success of those messages prompted an advertising agency executive to conjecture that a truly sophisticated, professionally-developed counteradvertising campaign could have an enormous impact on deterring smoking.[91]

Throughout the country are many other groups that work to reduce the burdens of smoking as either a singular focus or one of several health goals.* Each, in its own way, has enlarged the public's awareness and understanding of the smoking-and-health

---

* Prominent examples of grass-roots organizations dedicated exclusively to tobacco-and-health issues are Action on Smoking and Health (ASH), Americans for Nonsmokers' Rights (ANR), Group Against Smokers' Pollution (GASP), Citizens Against Tobacco Smoke (CATS), Stop Teenage Addiction to Tobacco (STAT), and the Tobacco Products Liability Project (TPLP).

issue. Yet each of these organizations possesses such modest resources that even collectively they cannot hope to compete with the multi-billion dollar tobacco industry for access to the public.

Organized Medicine

No group has responded to the smoking-and-health message more than American physicians. In the 1940s and 1950s, over 50 percent of physicians smoked, but since then the figure has dropped dramatically. In a recent survey of Rhode Island physicians, for example, researchers found a smoking prevalence of only 8.3 percent in 1983, down from 33 percent in 1963. Among physicians under age 30, the rate was only 4.5 percent.[12]

The role of the medical profession in transmitting its knowledge of smoking to the general population has been less exemplary. While many physicians conscientiously counsel their patients on smoking, many others do not. There is considerable irony in this since, on surveys, people claim that they would give up smoking, or would give it serious consideration, if their physicians told them to do so. While such statements might not translate into wholly consistent behavior, there is evidence from a controlled trial that physicians' counseling patients on smoking, even for only a couple of minutes, substantially increases the quit rate.[92] The irony of physicians' limited efforts in this area is that, for the time and effort invested, there are probably few things physicians can do that would have as substantial a long-run health impact.

With some noteworthy exceptions, the reticence of individual practitioners to deal with their patients' smoking has carried over to the roles of organized medicine in addressing the hazards of tobacco in the public forum. Certainly, the scientific arm of organized medicine has a long and illustrious history, as evidenced by the landmark publications on the hazards of smoking published in the *Journal of the American Medical Association* in the early 1950s. When one examines the organizational arm, however, the history is less illustrious. Over the years, for example, the American Medical Association has adopted a number of policy statements acknowledging the hazards of tobacco and urging reductions in its use, but its public pronouncements on the issue have been few and far between and relatively mild, until recently (as discussed below).

On occasion, a sinister element has crept into the AMA's dealings with tobacco. In 1984, for example, a reporter suggested that the AMA *Journal* had cancelled an article on tobacco it had previously accepted for fear of offending southern state legislators whom the Association needed for support on legislative matters.[93] The "sensitivity" of tobacco issues, in this political context, is illustrated by the text of a confidential memorandum distributed by the editor of *JAMA* to his editorial staff in 1982. Headed "Particularly Sensitive Political Issues," the memo read in part:

> In a recent meeting, [AMA Executive Vice-President] Doctor James Sammons and Mr. Thomas Hannon pointed out the existence of some particularly sensitive political questions and urged that we exercise appropriate caution in our JAMA publication on these subjects. They are:
>
> • tobacco and control of tobacco use,
> • nuclear war,
> • abortion
>
> . . . [S]ensitivities here are particularly high prior to the meetings of the Board of Trustees and . . . of the House of Delegates.[94]

When organized medicine has had an ideal opportunity to present the hazards of smoking to the public, it has not invariably insisted on its right to do so. Perhaps the most notorious episodes in this connection were a series of special supplements on personal health care written by the AMA and the American Academy of Family Physicians (AAFP) for, respectively, *Newsweek* and *Time* magazines. With one exception (in four supplements published from 1983 through 1985), the subject of smoking was not addressed at all, while full text pages were devoted to such topics as nutrition, diet, stress management, and exercise. Both the magazines and the medical associations offered lame explanations for the absence of discussion of smoking; but there is written evidence that the magazines resisted any mention of smoking, apparently for fear of offending advertisers. Obviously, the medical associations accepted this restriction, although, following substantial criticism from the health community, the AAFP did not prepare a second supplement for *Time* when the magazine refused to guarantee editorial control to the Association.[95]

32

These episodes created a furor within the public health and medical communities.[96] Criticism directed at the medical societies may have contributed to a new public aggressiveness by the medical community on the issue of tobacco and health. Over a recent period of 15 months, for example, *JAMA* produced three all-tobacco issues.[97-99] In late 1985, the AMA issued a call for a legal ban on promotion of tobacco products. While other health organizations had previously taken this position, the AMA's stature, and its willingness to make its view highly visible, brought the possibility to the public's attention in a manner that no previous organization's declaration could have. At present, the AMA and other elements of organized medicine are providing leadership on tobacco and health issues that has long seemed their logical role.

The first of *JAMA*'s three all-tobacco issues appeared after publication of a highly acclaimed all-tobacco issue of the *New York State Journal of Medicine*.[100] This and its successor tobacco issue[101] are worthy of note not only for their specific content, which was unusually political for a medical journal, but also as an "Establishment" accomplishment of their creator, former editor Dr. Alan Blum. An outspoken critic of the tobacco industry, particularly on the issue of advertising, Blum is also the founder and first president of DOC (Doctors Ought to Care), an anti-establishment group of physicians who develop satirical counteradvertising to emphasize the absurdity of the imagery of health and vitality that dominates cigarette advertising.* Once again, the financial resources available to DOC are minuscule, but the organization has substituted cleverness for money to promote its cause. DOC has created media events to generate the kind of publicity that the organization cannot afford to purchase directly. A prominent example is their sponsorship of the Emphysema Slims Tennis Tournament as a counterpoint to the Virginia Slims Tournament.

School Health Education

Most health professionals agree that the ultimate conquest of tobacco-related disease can only be achieved through primary prevention—preventing children from initiating tobacco habits. Tobacco's tenacious grip on its users means that cessation is not

---

* An example of a DOC ad is a macho male with his shirt partially unbuttoned, revealing a thick mat of black hair, and a cigarette stuck in his nose. The caption on the ad reads, "I smoke for smell."

a viable option for many; for others, much damage has already been inflicted once cessation can be achieved. Thus, a great deal of attention is properly focused on teaching children about tobacco. Less clear has been how to teach children so that they will retain what they have learned and, later, convert that knowledge into behavior as adolescents and adults. Many proponents of prevention have nevertheless been skeptics about the ability to undertake meaningful school health education on tobacco.

Recently, a major research effort provided evidence that school health education can translate into desired behavioral impact later in children's lives.[102] Publication of these findings should help resolve the debate within the public health community, but the effect on the actual provision of educational services is less probable. School health education in general suffers from competing demands on teachers' time and the restricted resource base of most public education systems. Assessments of the coverage of topics like tobacco and health in the nation's school systems suggest that the topics receive lip service in many systems, but few provide truly substantial curricula.

Regardless of our ability to assess their precise impacts, the nationwide efforts to educate children about the perils of smoking have produced a generation of children who are more sophisticated than were their parents at a comparable age; and many of their parents were elementary school students when the smoking-and-health message was made public in the 1950s and 1960s. The payoff to the educational effort would seem to be evident in the declining rates of smoking among teenagers; but several factors muddy these waters. Among them is the relative increase in smoking by girls and the increase in the use of smokeless tobacco by boys. Furthermore, it is impossible to say with any certainty that decreases in smoking are attributable to school health education, rather than to basic changes in the social environment regarding the acceptability of smoking. Regardless of the ultimate interpretation, it seems clear that school health education is and will remain a cornerstone of this nation's effort to produce a citizenry well informed about the leading cause of preventable premature death.

The "Other Side" of Publicity and Public Education

This section has reviewed the public's major sources of information on tobacco and health. There has been one omission, however, a source of disinformation that may well be more significant than any of those covered. The omission—tobacco advertising and related efforts—is the subject of the remaining chapters, following the next two sections' assessment of the sophistication of the public's understanding of the hazards of smoking. In examining that understanding, it is essential to recognize that it *has* been influenced by the tobacco industry. From the earliest years of "health scare" to the present, the industry has used advertising, quasi-advertising, and news releases to downplay the risks of smoking, to confuse and mislead the public. While it is impossible to assess the contribution of this disinformation to the public's limited appreciation of smoking's risks, it seems equally implausible to discount that campaign as a factor.

Public Understanding of the Hazards of Smoking

The call for a ban on tobacco advertising and promotion reflects in part advocates' belief that the public's understanding of tobacco's hazards is inadequate, and that massive expenditure on the promotion of tobacco products bears much of the responsibility. Before considering how cigarette advertising and promotion might influence consumer knowledge, we briefly examine the nature of the knowledge base.

The conventional wisdom is that everyone understands the basic facts of smoking and health. The logic underlying this conclusion is hard to challenge: that smoking is dangerous to health has been known, publicly, for three decades and the message has been conveyed to the public repeatedly through a wide variety of mechanisms. The product package itself is clearly labeled.

Survey findings support the conventional wisdom at its most superficial level. On one survey after the next, respondents acknowledge that smoking is hazardous to health and causes cancer. While nonsmokers exhibit greater recognition of these facts, the vast majority of smokers acknowledge them as well.

Despite this, surveys that have probed the depth of the public's knowledge have produced some startling findings indicating that understanding is remarkably superficial—for example, that recognition of smoking as "dangerous" does not necessarily translate into understanding that smoking reduces life expectancy. While the vast majority of survey respondents acknowledge smoking as a cause of cancer, sizable minorities of respondents do not recognize smoking as the principal cause of lung cancer; and a majority do not think of lung cancer as being typically fatal. Knowledge of the relationship between smoking and heart disease—the principal smoking-related killer—and smoking and chronic obstructive lung disease is "soft". And as would be expected, understanding erodes further once one gets beyond the most basic facts. For example, comprehension of the dangers of smoking during pregnancy is limited, and there is a great deal of misunderstanding of the implications of smoking low tar and nicotine cigarettes.[80]

The superficiality of the public's knowledge can be summarized as follows: for sizable percentages of the population, knowledge of the basic facts of smoking and health is exceedingly basic and the implications of those facts are not well understood. Furthermore, the public ranks smoking as a hazard in the same category as toxic dumps, saccharine, EDB in muffin mix, moderate overweight, and so on. That is, there is little differentiation of the *degree* of hazard, and hence the importance of not smoking becomes diluted by the perception that smoking is simply one more ingredient in an environmental soup of risks to health. Finally, careful research has revealed that smokers do not personalize the risks of smoking. They acknowledge them, but they perceive them to be "other people's problems."[80]

The issue of the superficiality of the public's understanding was brought forcefully to the attention of the smoking-and-health community in 1981 by a Federal Trade Commission staff report on an investigation of cigarette advertising.[80] In assessing the nature and depth of the public's knowledge of the hazards of smoking, the FTC staff relied heavily on the findings of eight survey studies, most previously conducted for other organizations, private and public, and the remainder commissioned by the FTC. To demonstrate the superficiality of the public's understanding, at least during the years 1978-80 when these surveys were conducted, we review some of the major findings cited in the public version of the FTC report.

Overall Risk of Smoking

- While 90 percent of survey respondents recognized that smoking is hazardous to health, from a fifth to a fourth of heavy smokers did not know this.
- In a 1980 Roper poll, 30 percent of all respondents and 41

36

percent of smokers did not know that a typical thirty-year-old man shortens his life expectancy *at all* by smoking.

- Among respondents who recognized that life expectancy was shortened, nonsmokers underestimated the loss of life expectancy (six to eight years) by two years; smokers underestimated it by four years.
- Half of the 1978 Roper poll respondents, and fully two-thirds of the smokers, did not conclude that smoking made "a great deal of difference" in life expectancy.
- Close to a third of the 1978 Roper respondents, including 40 percent of smokers, believed that "only heavy smoking is hazardous."
- In an FTC-commissioned study in 1979, two times as many respondents ranked traffic accidents as causing the most deaths during the previous year as chose smoking. In fact, for every traffic accident death, seven or eight people die from diseases caused by smoking.
- 90 percent underestimated the yearly number of smoking deaths, with more people selecting the lowest alternative—10,000 deaths—than the correct answer of 300,000.

Cancer

- In a 1978 Gallup poll, nearly one in five respondents did not believe that smoking causes lung cancer.
- In a 1980 Roper poll, 43 percent of respondents, including almost half of all smokers (49 percent), did not know that smoking causes most cases of lung cancer.
- When asked whether they agreed that "Air pollution is the major cause of lung cancer, not cigarette smoking," half of the respondents to a 1978 Roper study either agreed with the statement or answered "don't know."
- Half of a Chilton survey estimated that 25 or 45 percent of the victims of lung cancer die from the disease. In fact, 95 percent do, 70 percent within the first year and 90 percent within five years.
- Two-thirds of the 1980 Roper sample did not know that smoking causes most cases of cancer of the mouth.
- Three-quarters of the adults surveyed by Chilton did not believe that smoking was associated with bladder cancer. Smokers have a bladder cancer risk twice that of nonsmokers.

Heart Disease

- A third of 1978 Gallup poll respondents, including 40 percent of smokers of a pack or more per day, did not know that smoking caused heart disease.
- In the 1980 Roper study, two-thirds of respondents did not list smoking when asked in an open-ended question to name all the causes of heart attack of which they could think.*

Chronic Obstructive Lung Disease

- Almost 60 percent of the 1980 Roper sample did not know that smoking causes most cases of emphysema.
- Over a third did not know that smoking causes many cases of the disease.

Smoking and Pregnancy**

- Nearly half of the women polled by Roper in 1980 did not know that, "If a woman smokes during pregnancy, she significantly increases her risk of losing the baby before or during birth."
- Only 12 percent of the women polled mentioned smoking in response to an open-ended question to identify all of the causes of miscarriage of which they could think.
- Large minorities of the respondents to the Chilton survey did not appreciate the existence of the greater risks of miscarriage and stillbirth that are associated with smoking during pregnancy. Among smokers, the proportions ignorant of these effects of smoking reached and exceeded half.
- In a study of college students, almost three-quarters of the sample did not know that women who smoke during pregnancy have a significantly increased risk of spontaneous abortion or miscarriage.

---

* Knowledge of the smoking-heart disease connection may be improving considerably. On a recent survey, 90 percent of respondents agreed that smoking contributes to heart disease.[103] This does not address how "hard" this knowledge is, however.

** The findings reported here are from surveys predating or coinciding with publication of the 1980 Surgeon General's report on the health consequences of smoking for women.[43] The report devoted considerable attention to the effects of smoking on pregnancy. Publicity on these effects generated by media coverage of the report's issuance is not reflected in these findings.

- Over 60 percent of the students doubted or disbelieved that smoking reduces average birthweight.

Other Issues

- In the 1978 Roper sample, half of respondents felt that smoking was merely a habit, and not an addiction.
- In the Chilton and 1980 Roper studies, half or more of respondents did not know that cigarette smoke contains carbon monoxide.
- In the 1980 Roper survey, more than a third of smokers believed the statement that "It has been proven that smoking low-tar, low-nicotine cigarettes does not significantly increase a person's risk of disease over that of a nonsmoker." An additional third indicated that they did not know whether or not the statement was true.

Public Understanding: Concluding Observations

At the beginning of this section, we stated that the public acknowledges smoking as hazardous but ranks it simply as "one more ingredient in an environmental soup" of health risks. A single survey finding vividly illustrates the overall trivialization of the risks of smoking in the public's mind. When asked to identify the nation's most important health and safety measures, health and safety experts ranked not smoking as the number one priority. The general public, by contrast, ranked not smoking number ten.[104] Ranked ahead of not smoking were such items as having smoke detectors in the home, despite the fact that 6000 people die in home fires each year, while some 350,000 perish from smoking. Ironically, 30 percent or more of home fire deaths are the result of cigarette-ignited fires. The cigarette is the single most important cause of fires.[49]

The message of the data is that the public's understanding of tobacco's hazards is indeed surprisingly superficial. That superficiality has two important dimensions. First is the fact that the public has little appreciation of *how* hazardous smoking is. Second is the conclusion that many smokers, and presumably potential smokers, do not see the personal relevance of the dangers of smoking. The data contradict the assessment that further public education on the hazards of smoking is unnecessary, an assessment based on the premise that "everyone knows that smoking is bad for you." That most everyone acknowledges that smoking is hazardous is a tribute to the effectiveness of public education and publicity; that the level of understanding is so poor is an index of the difficulty of conveying the message and of the need to develop more effective methods for doing so.

The poverty of understanding may also be a reflection of the power of the tobacco industry's advertising and promotion activities. To the extent that cigarette advertisements successfully translate their imagery into consumer beliefs—acceptance of smoking as a normal everyday part of a healthy lifestyle—surely the message of cigarette ads at least partially offsets the message of health educators. But regardless of the specific effectiveness of the ads, their very presence—their acceptance by government and society—serves as a subliminal message that "Smoking can't be really all that dangerous; otherwise the government would ban cigarette advertising." When presented with that statement in a British government survey, 44 percent of smokers agreed.[105]

Implications of Public Understanding

That public knowledge of smoking's hazards has improved over the past quarter century is self-evident. It is reflected in the fact that the population of smokers represents the lowest precentage in decades, and adult per capita cigarette consumption, which has fallen annually since 1973, is now 22 percent below its 1963 peak and 40 percent below the level that might have been expected absent the antismoking campaign.[87] The rate of per capita consumption in 1985 was the lowest level attained since 1944 and represented a still more profound change than these numbers can indicate: the per capita consumption of *tobacco* had achieved its lowest level in a century.* That the transmission of the facts of smoking and health has been incomplete is reflected in the paucity of specific understanding and in the fact that tens of millions of Americans continue to smoke and hundreds of thousands of teenagers start to smoke each year.

---

* In addition to reflecting reductions in smoking, the record low use of tobacco results from the greater efficiency with which cigarettes are made today—there is less wastage and more parts of the tobacco plant are used—and the fact that less tobacco is used in the modern cigarette than in its predecessors. In 1954, 2.7 pounds of tobacco were used to make 1000 cigarettes. Today, only 1.7 pounds are needed for the same output.[106]

The picture, thus, is of the proverbial half-filled cup. Whether one views the cup as half empty or half full may reflect one's basic emotional predisposition as much as the inherent facts of the situation. It is important to appreciate these facts, however, to evaluate the implications of information—positive and negative— on the knowledge, attitudes, and behavior of smokers and potential smokers. As noted at the outset of this monograph, a major thesis is that these four phenomena are integrally related, that information influences knowledge, that knowledge change translates into attitudinal change, and that attitudinal change eventually develops into behavioral change.

Thus far we have reviewed how knowledge of smoking and health has evolved in the three decades since the media first delivered the science of smoking and health to the general public. We have briefly examined some of the behavioral changes that have redefined the size and composition of the smoking population. In closing this chapter, it seems useful to emphasize that the generalized knowledge change documented above has significantly altered the public's attitudes toward smoking. Since the mid-1960s, one survey after another has demonstrated that Americans are becoming less tolerant of public smoking, more insistent on their right to breathe air unpolluted by tobacco smoke.[107-109] The most significant manifestation of this attitudinal change has been the recent profusion of clean indoor air laws passed at the state and local level. Surveys even find a majority of smokers in favor of such laws.[110]

The attitudinal shift has not been uniform across all segments of society. While smoking exacts a social stigmatization in professional circles, it is still easily tolerated and is even the norm in many working class settings. It seems reasonable to characterize the change in the social acceptability of smoking over the past three decades as nothing short of profound; but it is vital to recognize that it is least profound in precisely those populations in which the knowledge change has been most superficial.

The behavioral changes noted above reinforce the perception that health behavior improvement is a product of increases in knowledge and derivative changes in attitudes toward risk factors. The two principal sources of information on smoking have both conveyed their messages through the media. One is reporting and commentary on the facts of smoking and health. The second is cigarette advertising. We have examined the former earlier in this chapter and will return to it, in a different context. Now we turn to the most prevalent form of information on cigarettes: advertising and promotion of the product.

CHAPTER 4

NATURE AND MAGNITUDE OF CIGARETTE ADVERTISING AND PROMOTION*

Magnitude and Distribution

The common, everyday cigarette—some chemically-treated plant material rolled inside a thin piece of paper, all of which costs only a penny or so to make—is the object of one of the most massive advertising and promotional campaigns that has ever been mounted. In 1984, the six major cigarette manufacturers devoted over $2 billion to encourage the use of their products.[5] Put into more readily comprehensible terms, expenditures on cigarette advertising and promotion amounted to almost $9 for every man, woman, and child in the United States. Alternatively, if one accepts the manufacturers' claim that their efforts are directed solely at capturing shares of a fixed market of existing smokers, the industry spent in the vicinity of $38 for every smoker.

Table 5 shows expenditures on cigarette advertising and (where available) promotion since 1970 in nominal amounts and, for total expenditures, in constant 1984 dollars. The most striking development is the shift from broadcast advertising in 1970 to print advertising beginning in 1971,** the result of the banning of

---

* Emphasis in this monograph is on the contemporary situation. The fascinating older history can be found in numerous previous writings.[17,111-114]

** The figures shown in Table 5 are illustrative of advertising spending patterns through most of the 1960s. TV and radio advertising expenditures peaked in 1967, when they totaled $244.4 million. Total pre-1970 ad expenditures also peaked that year, at $311.5 million. The relative constancy of expenditure totals and patterns in the five years immediately preceding the broadcast ad ban is seen in total expenditures varying only between $297.5 million and $311.5 million, with TV and radio expenditures constituting exactly 77 or 78 percent of the total for each year 1966 through 1969. In 1970, the TV/radio share dropped to 69 percent of the total and newspaper and magazine ad expenditures increased by almost a third over the preceding year. It seems likely that this relative shift represented a tentative step in the direction of the "brave new world" of cigarette advertising that was to emerge the following year. As Table 5 shows, newspaper and magazine expenditures in 1971 were two and one-half times those of 1970. As a share of total advertising, the newspaper and magazine expenditures rose from a fifth in 1970 to almost two-thirds in 1971.

advertising beginning in 1971,** the result of the banning of broadcast advertising of cigarettes, effective January 2, 1971, by the Public Health Cigarette Act of 1969.⁸⁷ At the hearings preceding passage of the Act, the president of one of the major tobacco companies stated that, in the event of a broadcast ad ban, he could not imagine the absolute amount of advertising reaching its earlier level, since television was by far the most effective advertising medium.[115] In fact, as the figures in Table 5 show, total nominal advertising expenditures exceeded those of the last year of broadcast advertising a mere five years later, and real (constant dollar) advertising and promotional expenditures caught up with the 1970 total only one year later.

Two general trends are also worthy of attention. One is the consistent substantial growth in real expenditures since the mid-1970s: from 1975 through 1983, total real expenditures increased by more than 18 percent per year. The other trend is the shift in locus of expenditures among the advertising media and between advertising and nonadvertising promotional activities. Among the advertising media, magazines and newspapers have remained the dominant locus of expenditures since the broadcast ad ban, although their relative dominance has decreased, from 62.6 percent of total advertising expenditures in 1971 to 54.5 percent in 1983.* During that time, while magazine and newspaper expenditures increased less than four-fold, other advertising expenditures more than quintupled.

The shift in the relative shares of advertising and promotional expenditures is pronounced. In 1970, the final year of broadcast advertising, fully 87 percent of the total was devoted to advertising. In the first post-ban year for which data on promotional expenditures are available, 1975, advertising accounted for three-quarters of all advertising and promotional expenditures. Since then, the advertising share has fallen steadily, to the point that in 1983 it represented only 57 percent of the total. Promotional expenditures, now verging on $1 billion by themselves, represent almost as large a real investment today as the grand total of advertising and

---

* Not seen in Table 5, due to the aggregation of magazine and newspaper expenditures, is the recent shift away from the latter. According to FTC data, in 1981 newspaper ad expenditures were 23 percent greater than those for magazines; newspaper expenditures totaled $358 million in 1981. Just two years later, newspaper ad expenditures were only half of magazine expenditures, the newspaper total having plummeted to $201 million.

Table 5. Cigarette Advertising and Promotional Expenditures, 1970–83 ($ millions)

Year	Advertising					Promotional (6)	Total (7) = (5) + (6)	Total in constant (1983) dollars (8)	Advertising as % of Total (9) = (5) ÷ (7)
	TV/radio (1)	Magazines & Newspapers (2)	Outdoor & transit (3)	Other (4)	Total (5)				
1970	217.4	64.2	11.7	21.4	314.7	46.3	361.0	962.2	87.2
1971	2.2	157.6	60.6	31.2	251.6	NA	NA	NA	NA
1972	—0—	159.2	67.5	30.9	257.6	NA	NA	NA	NA
1973	—0—	157.7	63.2	26.6	247.5	NA	NA	NA	NA
1974	—0—	195.1	71.4	40.3	306.8	NA	NA	NA	NA
1975	—0—	235.7	95.2	35.3	366.2	125.1	491.3	909.5	74.5
1976	—0—	263.8	122.0	44.2	430.0	209.1	639.1	1118.5	67.3
1977	—0—	364.0	141.8	46.2	552.0	247.5	799.5	1314.4	69.0
1978	—0—	371.2	171.9	57.4	600.5	274.5	875.0	1336.2	68.6
1979	—0—	498.7	184.2	66.1	749.0	334.4	1083.4	1487.1	69.1
1980	—0—	530.6	219.5	79.8	829.9	412.4	1242.3	1502.0	66.8
1981	—0—	649.3	250.0	99.0	998.3	549.4	1547.7	1695.4	64.5
1982	—0—	632.1	291.0	117.0	1040.1	753.7	1793.8	1851.5	58.0
1983	—0—	589.0	321.9	170.1	1081.0	819.8	1900.8	1900.8	56.9

Source:
Federal Trade Commission: Report to Congress Pursuant to the Federal Cigarette Labeling and Advertising Act, for the Years 1982–1983. Washington, DC: FTC, June 1985, as revised December 1985, Tables 6–8.

45

promotional expenditures did in 1970. The importance of this phenomenon is substantial in the context of the inquiry into the impacts of cigarette advertising and promotion and the policy debate over whether to ban them. Only a few years ago, the health community generally did not recognize the role of nonadvertising promotional expenditures, as was reflected in the early calls for bans: virtually all of them focused exclusively on advertising. Awareness of promotional expenditures received a substantial boost in 1984 with the publication of *Smoke Ring*,[116] a book that discussed their magnitude and institutional implications.

As the figures in Table 5 suggest, the importance of promotional efforts is rising exceedingly rapidly in the most recent years. From 1980 to 1983, for example, total advertising expenditures rose 30 percent. During the same three-year period, promotional expenditures doubled. Recently, the president of Brown & Williamson Tobacco Company predicted that promotional expenditures will exceed advertising expenditures by a factor of four by 1990.[117] Consistent with this prospect is industry discussion of the need to scrutinize magazine advertising more carefully, reducing its overall share of advertising and promotion expenditures and targeting it away from "high-brow" and "middle-brow" publications and toward those with a greater blue collar readership.[118] Blacks are also being targeted more aggressively.[10]

Advertising

Nature of Cigarette Advertising

Few images rival the Marlboro Man for familiarity. This and the other images of cigarette ads are seen daily by virtually every American. The images are encountered when flipping through almost every major magazine and when driving on the highway: no other product commands as much space on the nation's billboards as the cigarette.

Regarding the imagery of cigarette ads, it is instructive to identify the principal categories of ad themes and juxtapose them against a voluntary advertising code the cigarette manufacturers adopted in 1964 in response to the adverse publicity associated with the Surgeon General's report. The code specified that "cigarette advertising shall not represent that cigarette smoking is essential to social prominence, distinction, success or sexual attraction," and that it not be associated with vigorous physical activity. The manufacturers also agreed to use only models over age 25 and to avoid advertising intended to appeal to children and teenagers, then defined as persons under 21 years of age.[115]

The code is honored today mostly in the breach. The image of social prominence and distinction seems to be the central message emanating from the tuxedo-clad Barclay smoker and is embedded in the appeal to the first "designer cigarette," Ritz, associated with the famous "YSL" logo of Yves Saint Laurent. While the concept of a "designer cigarette" is new, the appeal to high fashion, stylishness, and social acceptability represents a return to an earlier imagery. In addition to Barclay and Ritz, the theme is seen in ads for Players, Satin, and Benson and Hedges.

The theme of success is spelled out explicitly, in writing, in Vantage ads that herald "the taste of success." The sexual attraction of the provocatively dressed models in recent ads for Luckies is flagrant. As if the models' expressions and attire were not sufficiently alluring, the models say, "Light my Lucky." One of them is a bare-chested young male who might be judged too young to order a beer in a bar.

The association with vigorous physical activity is explicit in a series of Kent ads in which the model is "cooling down" after a hard game of tennis or some other racket sport, a cigarette serving to relax the triumphant athlete. Similarly, Vantage shows a model engaging in a vigorous dance, perhaps a demanding ballet, and Sterling portrays a model hang-gliding.

Cigarette ad themes transcend the short list originally prohibited by the code. A common theme today is independence, possibly best reflected in a series of ads for Camels in which the rugged Camel man relaxes with his smoke atop a mountain peak, in a remote forest, or in a Third World country. These ads' image of independence is diametrically opposite to reality: most smokers are typically enticed to smoke by a need to conform and soon thereafter become highly dependent on their cigarettes.

Closely related to the independence theme is, for want of a better word, the macho theme. Here rides the pervasive Marlboro Man and his latter-day counterpart, the Kool motorcyclist, his two-wheeler clenched tightly between his legs and roaring down the highway next to the beach. It is interesting to note, parenthetically, that while they are lit, the Marlboro Man's and the Kool cyclist's cigarettes emit no smoke. Smoke is rarely seen in cigarette ads because it conveys a negative image, especially in an era of consciousness of nonsmokers' rights. Advertisers air-brush smoke out of cigarette ads.

A major theme of recent years, best exemplified by the Virginia Slims ads, is the notion that smoking is associated with independence for women, with women's liberation. The theme has been immortalized in the Virginia Slims ads' imagery and in their slogan, "You've come a long way, baby!" In fact, of course, the exact opposite is true: the female smoker has merely conformed to the previously male standard of smoking, thereby chaining herself to the nation's most deadly habit. As observers of trends in women's cigarette advertising have paraphrased the slogan, "You've come the wrong way, baby!"

While the above ads are likely familiar to all readers, there are numerous ads that are unfamiliar to many of us because they are placed in publications and on billboards directed at specific minority groups. Most white people are unfamiliar with major ad campaigns targeted at blacks and Hispanics, for example.

Finally, a theme that was prevalent from the early 1970s through the early 1980s, accompanying the growth in low t/n cigarettes, was the "health theme." In various guises, this theme has popped up at several points throughout the century. While the message and the method have changed, the health theme ad has always represented an attempt to portray smoking, or smoking the advertised brand, as somehow "safe" or at least "less hazardous."[69,111,119]

Today, the low t/n cigarette is the dominant product on the market, but the health theme ad has become uncommon, perhaps because it is viewed as counterproductive, reminding smokers of the risk to which they are exposing themselves.[111] A few cigarette brands still rely on it, such as Now, which emphasizes its low-tar rating. Other low t/n cigarettes have shed the health theme imagery, returning to the more conventional images of the "virtues" of cigarettes; these include True, Merit, and Vantage, to name only a few. Even the prototypical modern low t/n cigarette, Carlton, relies only subtly on the health theme. Its current ad states, simply, "If you smoke, please try Carlton." One must assume that the reason is clear; but it is also implicit.

Institutional Significance of Cigarette Advertising

As Peter Taylor has documented in *Smoke Ring*, tobacco advertising and promotional expenditures have numerous, subtle, and important influences on a wide variety of national institutions, ranging from the press to government, from organized sport to organized medicine.[116] One of the most significant, and insidious, is the effect of cigarette advertising revenues on the media's coverage of smoking and health. The potential influence of these revenues is seen in Tables 6 and 7, which present advertising revenues for several major magazines in selected recent years, in both absolute dollar amounts and, where data were readily available, as a percent of total advertising revenue for the publications. Table 6 includes general interest magazines and a few specialty publications, while Table 7 covers only major women's magazines.* The figures indicate that many of the nation's most prominent magazines received substantial fractions of their advertising revenues from cigarette ads. The tables also indicate that a few prominent magazines received no revenue from cigarette ads, the result of conscious decisions to refuse to accept cigarette ads. While various health groups have identified over 100 publications

---

* The reason to list the women's magazines separately is that, as a group, they have been identified as providing the worst coverage of smoking and health. This is discussed in the next chapter.

Table 6. Advertising Revenues for Selected General Interest and Specialty Magazines, 1980 or 1981

| Magazine | Year | Cigarette ad revenue | |
		$ millions	% total
Time	1981	40.5	17.2
Parade	1981	36	25.4
Newsweek	1981	30	15.8
TV Guide	1980	27	n.a.
Sports Illustrated	1980	21	n.a.
People	1980	15.5	n.a.
U.S. News & World Report	1981	11	14.6
Playboy	1980	9.5	n.a.
Field & Stream	1980	4	n.a.
Popular Mechanic	1980	3	n.a.
Car & Driver	1980	1.5	n.a.
Reader's Digest	1981	0	0
New Yorker	1981	0	0

Sources:
Dale KC: ACSH survey: which magazines report the hazards of smoking? ACSH News and Views 1982; 3(3): 8–9; and Hutchings R: A review of the nature and extent of cigarette advertising in the United States. National Conference on Smoking or Health—Developing a Blueprint for Action. New York, NY: American Cancer Society, 1981, pp. 255–256.

49

Table 7. Advertising Revenues for Selected Women's Magazines, 1984

Magazine	Cigarette ad revenue	
	$ millions	% total
Family Circle	16.3	12.5
Better Homes & Gardens	15.0	11.9
Woman's Day	13.8	12.5
McCall's	10.7	14.0
Ladies' Home Journal	9.3	14.0
Redbook	8.0	15.1
Cosmopolitan	7.5	7.9
Vogue	3.6	5.4
Harper's Bazaar	2.8	8.8
Mademoiselle	2.5	6,8
Ms.	0.5	7.9
Good Housekeeping	0	0
Seventeen	0	0

Source:
Ernster VE: Mixed messages for women: a social history of cigarette smoking and advertising. NY State J Med 1985; 85:339.

that refuse cigarette ads, only a handful of the country's major magazines fall into this category.

Several of the magazines in Tables 6 and 7 include large readerships among teenagers (e.g., *TV Guide*, *Sports Illustrated*, *People*, *Playboy*, *Car & Driver*, *Family Circle*, *Cosmopolitan*). The cigarette companies claim that their advertising is directed solely at adults, and at confirmed smokers among the adults. These data, and the youthful imagery of the ads found in many of these magazines, challenge this claim, as does common sense and additional evidence, both discussed below.

Magazines' dependence on cigarette ad revenues is substantially greater than that of newspapers. Newspaper revenues from cigarette ads often run on the order of one to three percent of total revenues. For major newspapers, this can amount to a substantial dollar figure; but the proportional dependence on cigarette ads is certainly much less than that of major magazines. To illustrate, in 1984 the *Washington Post* received $2.1 million in cigarette advertising revenues, which amounted to two-thirds of one percent of total ad revenue for the year.[120] Among the reasons for the relatively smaller role of cigarette ads in newspapers' advertising revenues are the fact that so much of newspaper advertising is of a local character, since most newspapers serve a local readership, and the fact that the imagery of cigarette ads is best served by a glossy colorful presentation, which newsprint does not deliver.

As substantial as the magazine ad dollars may be, they considerably understate the publications' economic dependence on the cigarette makers. Each of the cigarette companies is a conglomerate, and the products produced by these conglomerates cover the full range of everyday consumer goods. The pervasiveness of the cigarette companies' control of consumer products is such that it is the very rare American who does not use a cigarette company product each and every day. A short list of some of the common household-name products sold by the cigarette companies will make this point amply clear. These include Kentucky Fried Chicken, Dole Pineapple, Miller Beer, Lite Beer, Canada Dry, Shredded Wheat, Oreo Cookies, Jello, Bulova watches, Minute Rice, Ritz crackers, Planters Nuts, Cool Whip, Life Savers, Carefree gum, Sanka, Chun King, Oscar Mayer, Grape Nuts, Maxwell House coffee, Smirnoff vodka, Jim Beam, J & B Scotch, Ingelnook wines, and Smurfberry Crunch cereal.

The significance of the companies' diversification, in the present context, is that publications' dependence on advertising revenues from the cigarette companies extends well beyond revenues for cigarette ads per se. This is demonstrated vividly in the following data:

- In 1983, four of the six cigarette-producing conglomerates ranked in the top 10 among magazine advertisers. R.J. Reynolds ranked as the nation's leading magazine advertiser and Philip Morris ranked second.
- That same year, the same four companies ranked among the top 10 newspaper advertisers, with R.J. Reynolds again leading the list.
- The same four companies were the nation's top four outdoor advertisers.[121]

While the above figures suggest the enormity of the importance of the cigarette companies to the media, they preceded three of the most significant acquisitions ever achieved by the cigarette companies, or by any companies for that matter. In 1985, R.J. Reynolds acquired the Nabisco Company. Later in the year, Philip Morris acquired General Foods. The latter was the largest non-oil company merger in history. These acquisitions mean that in 1986 and ensuing years, each of R.J. Reynolds and Philip Morris, by itself, will be spending in the vicinity of $1 billion or more on advertising and promotion annually. Of lesser importance financially, but highly germane to a consideration of the influence of cigarette companies on the media, is the 1985 acquisition by Loew's Corp., the parent company of Lorillard, of a significant block of shares of CBS.

Promotion

Not all cigarette advertising comes in the form of commercials touting cigarettes in magazines and newspapers and on billboards. Numerous, diverse other forms of promotion are used to acquaint smokers, and potential smokers, with cigarette brands, or to generate an image of the cigarette maker as socially responsible, the proverbial pillar of the community. As defined by the Federal Trade Commission, nonadvertising promotional activities include sampling distribution, promotional allowances, distribution bearing name, distribution not bearing name, public entertainment, direct mail, endorsements, testimonials, audio-visual, etc.[5] Within these categories fall a wide range of activities, including such familiar ones as sponsorship of sports events and the arts, contests and give-aways, retail outlet promotions, and the street corner handing out of free samples of cigarettes. With the nonadvertising share of advertising and promotional expenditures increasing rapidly, it is important to appreciate the nature and significance of the emerging strategies to sell smoke to the American consumer.

Nature of Nonadvertising Promotional Activities

The data in Table 5 indicated that nonadvertising promotional expenditures for cigarettes are well on their way to becoming a $1 billion enterprise by themselves. Promotional efforts vary from handing out free cigarette samples at rock concerts to supporting fund-raising activities for local hospitals, with company or brand sponsorship often publicized. The category of "promotion" thus covers a diversity of types of activities united, definitionally, only by the fact that they are intended to enhance the sponsor's image or directly maintain and boost cigarette sales (in the aggregate or for individual brands) and are not conventional advertising.

Sampling distribution is a prominent promotional technique that is simple in concept and execution: a company is hired to distribute samples of particular cigarette brands, typically in mini-packs of a few cigarettes, to passersby either on the streets of a community or at special events. The cigarette companies claim that samples are given only to adults and that sampling distribution will not occur close to "centers of youth activity." Each of these "protections" is violated frequently, with numerous documented instances of samples having been handed to young teenagers and with sampling occurring close to schools and universities, as well as at such centers of youth activity as the aforementioned rock concerts. When individuals distributing cigarettes have been confronted about handing cigarettes to children, they refer their accusers to their managers, who in turn refer them to the cigarette company. The company's response commonly is that, while it adheres to the distribution guidelines, it has no control over what the local hired hands actually do.

Another familiar promotional device is the contest or give-away in which smokers are encouraged to enter a contest to win trips or prizes. Implicitly, such promotions associate cigarette brands, or cigarettes in general, with pleasant activities; undoubtedly, the manufacturer hopes that individuals will be enticed to smoke their brands through association with the contest.

A third familiar device, for which popularity has waxed and waned over time, is the awarding of coupons with packs or cartons of cigarettes. Coupons can be exchanged for a wide variety of consumer goods, even including an automobile, if one smokes enough (or at least buys enough cigarettes). One scholar has characterized this extreme "give-away" as "external combustion leading to internal combustion."[122]

Another increasingly familiar form of promotion is sponsorship of sports events. The prototypic case is the Virginia Slims Tennis Tournament, a tournament that is so widely recognized that "Virginia Slims" has become almost synonymous with women's professional tennis. But sports sponsorship extends to horse racing (e.g., the Marlboro Cup), car racing (again, Marlboro comes to mind, as does Skoal, among smokeless tobacco products), golf (Vantage), soccer (Winston), and so on. Sports sponsorship has a more micro form in the companies' paying athletes to wear their logos; a prominent case was tennis star Martina Navratilova's donning an outfit designed to resemble the packaging of Kim cigarettes, a British cigarette marketed to women.

Sports sponsorship represents one of the most ironic of the promotional techniques, in that few of the direct beneficiaries of the companies' largesse, the athletes themselves, would today dare to smoke, for smoking is wholly antithetical to fitness, endurance, and athletic performance. Sports sponsorship also represents an effective device for getting around the ban on broadcast advertising of cigarettes, since the sponsor's name is spoken and seen repeatedly whenever a sponsored sporting event is broadcast. The pervasiveness of the cigarette logo on broadcast sports events has led one British observer to estimate that the cigarette message may be receiving almost as much air time through such exposure today as it did through advertisements when the latter were permitted.[116]

Sponsorship extends to other areas of society that develop similar dependency on tobacco money to exist and thrive. The most prominent of these areas is music, with the Kool Jazz Festival perhaps the best known example. As in the case of sports, the irony is plentiful, with many jazz greats having been chain smokers and victims of lung cancer, such as Duke Ellington. Music sponsorship encompasses a range from support of the Farm Aid concert to support of symphony orchestras. Other cultural activities that have been the beneficiaries of tobacco industry support include art museums, ballet companies, and, for the ultimate irony, hospitals. An example of the latter was Virginia Slims' raising funds for Children's Hospital Medical Center in Oakland, California.

Still another form of sponsorship has been the industry's collaborating with professional organizations to produce and publicize an activity of interest to the organizations, but one which the organizations could not afford on their own. Tobacco industry support makes the activity feasible and may lend the tobacco industry an image of "wholesomeness" through the association with the otherwise socially desirable activity. A prominent recent example was the Tobacco Institute's funding of a booklet prepared by the National Association of State Boards of Education and entitled, "Helping Youth Decide." According to the introduction, the purpose of the booklet was to "help family members . . . make more responsible decisions . . . " The Tobacco Institute's role was acknowledged on the inside front cover as making the booklet possible. The Institute claimed that, "The people who make cigarettes do not want young people smoking them."[123]*

---

* This frequent industry claim led activist Elizabeth Whelan to ask the Tobacco Industry *why* they did not want children to smoke, since they continually deny that there is anything wrong with smoking.[124] The Institute did not respond to Whelan's inquiry.

Presumably, the benefit of sponsorship derives from the good will that is generated both within the benefitting organizations and among the public, who appreciate the work of the organizations and see the role of the tobacco industry in bringing it to them. Thus, sponsorship is undertaken with the intention, usually if not always, of making the public explicitly aware of the tobacco industry's largesse in making these "good works" possible.

In contrast, another form of "sponsorship" is done "behind the scenes," with the tobacco industry's role intentionally obscured or at least not made public. A prominent example was Philip Morris' alleged payment to the producers of the movie, *Superman II*, to show the Marlboro logo as part of the "scenery" of the movie. During *Superman II*, a movie directed to a significant degree to an audience of children, the Marlboro logo appeared frequently.[125] This is not an isolated event, although no one knows precisely how extensive is the practice of such "payola", plugging cigarettes through the subtle means of making the familiar logo part of an appealing back-drop.

One of the more intriguing forms of promotional effort in recent years has been "social issue advertising." This is an effort of the Tobacco Institute or an individual manufacturer to bring to the public's attention the cigarette industry's perspective on the social and scientific issues in smoking. The most recent major advertising campaign of this type has been the R.J. Reynolds Company's "open debate" ads, a series introduced to "encourage an open debate" on the issues when in fact Reynolds was the only side of the argument having the resources to buy media space to present its case. This series has ranged in scope and seriousness from a challenge to the conventional wisdom that smoking contributes to heart disease to a "cutesy" appeal to smokers not to smoke in bed. In between have been discussions of the inappropriateness of legislating restrictions on smoking in public places and claims that the scientific evidence does not support the conclusion that environmental tobacco smoke is hazardous to nonsmokers.

Noted earlier, the ad challenging the cardiovascular disease/ smoking connection is particularly interesting because it is one of the most obvious of recent industry efforts to allay smokers' fears about the hazards inherent in their habits.[64] The ad relies on the findings of a major government-funded health promotion intervention study—the Multiple Risk Factor Intervention Trial—to question the relationship between smoking and cardiovascular deaths.

The text of the ad misinterprets the findings of the study, which was not designed to assess that relationship and which nevertheless did find the familiar connection between smoking and heart disease deaths. The Federal Trade Commission has concluded that the ad was misleading.[65] Regardless, it seems likely that Reynolds has succeeded in persuading some smokers, who want to believe that their habits are not really "all that dangerous," that the basic facts of smoking and health are not as well-established as in fact they are.

The Reynolds series is similar in nature and purpose to an earlier campaign by the Tobacco Institute. In an ad entitled, "Do cigarette companies want kids to smoke?" the text began, "No. As a matter of policy. No. As a matter of practice. No. As a matter of fact. No!" To some observers, this representation is among the most cynical the industry offers, since, as noted earlier, the industry would lose its customers if children did not start smoking and become addicted.

The industry's sense of "balance" in presenting its message is illustrated by a full-page social-issue ad that was placed by Reynolds in major newspapers and magazines in 1984 in response to public concern about the dangers of involuntary smoking.[66] As described earlier, the ad relied heavily on the fact that one of "the tobacco industry's biggest critics," Lawrence Garfinkel of the American Cancer Society, had not found evidence of involuntary smoking lung cancer in a study based on U.S. data.[40] Garfinkel claimed that his findings were taken out of context, but while he stated this in a letter to the editor of the New York Times,[67] Reynolds' message filled an entire page of that newspaper, as well as numerous other publications. Not surprisingly, Reynolds did not publicize the more recent findings of Garfinkel and colleagues from a study designed specifically to address the link between involuntary smoking and lung cancer.[68] That study supported the conclusion of many early studies that substantial chronic exposure to tobacco smoke does increase the nonsmoker's risk of lung cancer.[41]

A further example of social issue advertising ran in several prominent liberal magazines in 1984. Headed "We're the tobacco industry, too," the ad featured a picture of three workers—a black man, a white man, and a white woman—who are members of the Bakery Confectionary and Tobacco Workers International Union. The text begins by describing how the union workers have participated actively in social causes, honoring the work of Martin Luther

King, Jr., and so on. The text then informs the reader that "well-meaning" but presumably misguided anti-smokers are threatening their jobs.[126] The appeal to liberal support for unions and unionism is clear, although it may well have back-fired. Noted supporters of liberal causes, including unionism, have labeled the ad one of the most exploitative efforts they have seen.[127,128] Their obvious concern is that the appeal for the tobacco workers' jobs must be juxtaposed against the deaths created by the product they produce, an exchange that can be estimated at roughly one job per year in exchange for one tobacco-related death.[129]

The remaining promotional techniques are numerous and diverse, ranging from publication of a guide to Hispanic organizations and their leaders, to seminars and conferences hosted by the industry in very posh settings for such groups as an association of black journalists, to financial contributions to legislators through conventional campaign-funding mechanisms and honoraria for lectures. In the latter category, in 1984 the tobacco industry paid more to congressmen in honoraria than any other interest group.

A novel effort is being mounted by Philip Morris to respond more aggressively to "the antismoking forces." This campaign includes publication of the new *Philip Morris Magazine*, a publication for smokers that features articles of general interest, discussions of pro-smoking efforts around the country, and criticism of anti-smoking activities. The campaign also includes insertion of a message in cartons of particular brands of cigarettes (e.g., More) warning smokers of their loss of freedoms from nonsmokers' rights laws, increasing excise taxes, etc.[130,131]

Institutional Significance of Cigarette Promotion

The institutional significance of cigarette promotion is difficult to assess quantitatively. While the Federal Trade Commission receives figures on promotional expenditures by the cigarette manufacturers, these are not broken down into sufficient detail to describe the financial role the industry plays in supporting the institutions considered above. However, a few comments of a qualitative nature can be made about the direct and indirect institutional significance of cigarette companies' promotional expenditures.

First and foremost, it is clear that no societal institution is so dependent on cigarette promotional dollars that the institution's

57

future would be jeopardized by withdrawl of those dollars. But, like the case of magazines' dependence on cigarette advertising revenues, individual members of several institutions might find their viability threatened. For example, the heavy dependence of some portions of American soccer and of women's professional tennis could mean that these sports would have to work hard to sustain their current levels of activity absent tobacco industry sponsorship. A model for the possibility of "life after tobacco sponsorship" has been provided by the experience of the Canadian Ski Association which decided after much debate, and pressure from the health community, to refuse to continue to accept tobacco industry sponsorship of Canadian ski events.

Similarly, several cultural events might be jeopardized, ranging from the Kool Jazz Festival to art exhibits. There is little doubt that cultural institutions derive significant support for their activities from tobacco sponsors; neither, however, is there doubt that jazz and art would survive without such money.

The potentially insidious role of tobacco industry largesse in funding legislators' campaigns, or simply providing them with income, and entertaining journalists is obvious yet difficult to assess. Certainly such activities must produce some reservoir of good will among the beneficiaries, and such good will might well be expected to color the way legislators, journalists, and others look at tobacco issues.

Perhaps the least well-defined but potentially most important institutional impact of cigarette companies' promotions is their contribution to creating an aura of legitimacy, of wholesomeness, for an industry that produces a product that annually accounts for about a fifth of all American deaths. The image of the tobacco industry is undoubtedly not pristine; but neither is it likely that most members of the general public, or of state and federal legislatures, subscribe to Ellen Goodman's characterization of the industry as "just a notch above . . . the streetcorner pusher."[132] Promotional expenditures undoubtedly serve in the aggregate to enhance and protect the industry's image as a valid, legitimate wheel in the machine of private enterprise, and likely to sell cigarettes as well. As the president and chief executive officer of R.J. Reynolds has put it, "We made it clear from the day we announced our sponsorship [of horse racing] that we were in the business of selling cigarettes, not the racing business."[133]

CHAPTER 5

FUNCTIONS OF CIGARETTE ADVERTISING:
THEORY AND EVIDENCE

Theory

Does cigarette advertising encourage smoking? In particular, does advertising encourage children to smoke? As would be expected, within the public health community there is a strong consensus that advertising does encourage smoking and that it is a significant influence on children's adopting the habit, although not necessarily the principal influence (and certainly not the only one). Industry representatives, on the other hand, unanimously claim that advertising does not affect smoking rates or levels. They contend that individual companies and individual brands are vying with each other simply for brand share, for larger slices of an economic pie of a fixed and independently determined size. The industry also contends that advertising serves the function of conveying useful information to smokers, such as brands' tar and nicotine ratings.

The argument over whether advertising affects smoking in the aggregate tends to obscure the issue of *how* advertising might affect smoking, if it does so at all. In fact, there are several quite separate ways in which advertising could affect consumption. Some of these are direct; that is, the advertising (its imagery, etc.) could directly encourage people to smoke or smokers to consume more cigarettes. In addition, there are indirect mechanisms by which advertising could influence something else (e.g., institutional behavior) which, in turn, affects smoking.

The direct mechanisms are four in number:

1. Advertising could entice children or young adults to experiment with cigarettes and initiate tobacco habits. This is the concern at the heart of opposition to cigarette advertising, since children are not deemed to be in a position to make mature, rational judgments about smoking.

2. Advertising could reduce current smokers' resolve to quit or to consider quitting. Repeatedly confronting the smoker with its glamorous imagery, and its implicit allaying of fears, advertising could blunt good intentions and motivation.

3. Advertising could increase current smokers' daily consumption of cigarettes. The imagery of ads could serve as an immediate cue, a stimulus, to smoke that reaches the smoker at a subconscious level.

4. Advertising could encourage former smokers to resume their habits. The seductive imagery of the ads could break the smoker's resolve to remain off of cigarettes. The quitter must grapple with both physiological and psychological withdrawl, and must do so in an environment in which there are many cues to smoke, reinforcing of the attractions of smoking.

These statements represent possibilities, not certainties, and it seems likely that to the extent that they are realities, they apply differently to different types of individuals.

The indirect mechanisms by which advertising might influence smoking are:

1. The media's dependence on advertising revenues from the cigarette companies may discourage full and open discussion of the hazards of tobacco use and of the workings of the industry. If this is the case, the public is receiving less information on the dangers of smoking than it would in an environment in which coverage was influenced solely by the inherent newsworthiness of the subject. Since we know that information on tobacco hazards has led to knowledge change, which in turn has been converted into behavior change, it follows that greater availability of information and commentary would lead to an even lower rate of smoking. Thus, while smoking rates in 1986 are well below those of the early 1960s, they are still high, in part due to the reluctance of the media to tackle the subject with the full force they would devote to a health hazard that was not the object of a billion-dollar advertising campaign.

2. Cigarette advertising may contribute to an environment in which smoking is perceived to be socially acceptable or at least "not really all that bad." It is easy to imagine how such an environment contributes to the initiation of smoking habits by children and helps to sustain habits among adult smokers.

Evidence

Direct Mechanisms

Does cigarette advertising directly encourage smoking that would not occur in its absence? The evidence on this question is diverse in type, ample in quantity but thin in quality, and often conflicting in its conclusions. The evidence falls into two categories: (1) logic and experience and (2) formal empirical analysis.

Logic and Experience. Advertising executives say that market expansion is invariably a purpose of advertising, even for a mature industry, and they note that few advertising experts claim that their trade serves exclusively a market-share function, except in a self-serving case like that of cigarettes. Emerson Foote, former chairman of the board of McCann-Erickson, the world's second largest advertising agency, once responsible for $20 million in cigarette accounts, put it this way: "[T]he cigarette industry has been artfully maintaining that cigarette advertising has nothing to do with total sales . . . [T]his is complete and utter nonsense. The industry knows it is nonsense . . . I am always amused by the suggestion that advertising, a function that has been shown to increase consumption of virtually every other product, somehow miraculously fails to work for tobacco products."[134]

No one would assert that market expansion is the *sole* function of advertising. Specific ad campaigns clearly appear to be targeted at brand share; witness the recent ads for Carlton cigarettes that say, simply, "If you smoke, please try Carlton." But overall advertising trends, both current and historical, make it difficult to believe that the intention of ad campaigns has been exclusively brand share. For example, among the most significant advertising trends in the past three decades has been the aggressive advertising of cigarettes marketed for women. The advertising campaign emerged well before, and led, the diffusion of the habit within the targeted group (women). It can be argued that the cigarette advertisers simply saw the coming trend and hopped on the advertising bandwagon to establish claims in a market that was emerging for other reasons. But to many students of the subject it seems implausible that the massive, "pre-emptive" ad campaign did not influence the amount of acceptance of the object of the advertising.[135]

That advertisers believe their efforts can recruit new smokers, among children, is vividly illustrated in an advertising strategy developed for the Brown & Williamson Company and revealed during the Federal Trade Commission's cigarette advertising investigation. The strategy, which Brown & Williamson claims it rejected, stated:

Thus, an attempt to reach young smokers, starters, should be based . . . on the following major parameters:

- Present the cigarette as one of a few initiations into the adult world.
- Present the cigarette as part of the illicit pleasure category of products and activities.
- To the best of your ability (considering some legal re-straints), relate the cigarette to 'pot', wine, beer, sex, etc.
- DON'T communicate health or health-related points.[136]

Two current advertising campaigns lend further support to the notion that market expansion is a goal of cigarette advertising. One is an expanding effort directed at the Hispanic community, with an increasing emphasis on Hispanic women, a group known to have a smoking prevalence well below average[11] and therefore considered an attractive marketing target. The second is the growing advertising effort of the tobacco multinationals in Third World countries. In many of these countries, relatively few people currently smoke manufactured cigarettes, so the proliferation of billboards and similar advertising associating smoking with so-phistication and affluence can only be directed at market expan-sion.[116,137,138]

In several countries in which cigarettes are a government monopoly, the state enterprise advertises. If advertising served solely to redistribute smokers among brands, there would be no reason to advertise in such countries, a point that an executive of a major British cigarette manufacturer has acknowledged.[139]

A logical argument in support of the conclusion that advertising does expand the market comes, ironically, from the Tobacco Institute's vocal opposition to the proposal to ban all cigarette advertising. If the only function of advertising were to determine brand share, as the industry claims, the Institute, representing all of the manufacturers, should have no practical basis for opposing an ad ban. To the contrary, if banning advertising did not decrease consumption (which is the corollary to the argument that advertising increases consumption), a ban would work simply to increase industry profits, reducing the companies' costs by over $1 billion per year (the after-tax cost of $2 billion in advertising and promotion expenditures), without reducing sales. Indeed, the argument that a ban would work principally to increase industry profits, at least in the short run, has both theory and experience (following the TV-radio ad ban) to support it, an issue to which we will return.

Of course, the Institute could (and does) argue that the industry opposes an ad ban on grounds of principle, appealing to the broad social implications of the makers of a legal product losing their right to advertise. This argument rings hollow, however, when one examines the history of the industry's position in the policy debate on removing cigarette ads from the nation's airwaves. In the late 1960s, industry representatives reportedly worked quietly to seek from Congress an exemption from antitrust action if the tobacco companies agreed to remove their cigarette advertising from TV and radio.[115] Their logic, confirmed by independent analysis,[83] was that the antismoking messages required by the Federal Communication Commission's Fairness Doctrine were discouraging smoking more than the pro-smoking ads were encouraging it. While the antitrust exemption was not granted, the desired effect was achieved in Congress' passage of the Public Health Cigarette Smoking Act of 1969 which banned cigarette advertising from the broadcast media. In short, the industry did not object on principle to a legal ban on advertising when the ban served the industry's economic purpose.

There are alternative explanations for the Tobacco Institute's opposition to the ad ban proposal. It is conceivable, for example, that the two major manufacturers, Philip Morris and R.J. Reynolds, controlling two-thirds of the total cigarette market, believe that an ad ban would work to their disadvantage in the brand-share battle; and that, given their dominance of the industry, these two firms have effective control of the Tobacco Institute's position on the issue. But this seems highly unlikely. Indeed, a ban might work to the relative advantage of these firms, as they have the established products and a ban would eliminate one avenue for competition to cut into their markets.

The industry itself provides an additional observation supporting a direct link between advertising and smoking. A Brown & Williamson marketing executive, quoted anonymously, told a reporter at the *Louisville Courier Journal* that:

Nobody is stupid enough to put it in writing, or even in words, but there is always the presumption that your marketing approach should contain some element of market expansion, and market expansion in this industry means two things—kids and women. I think that governs the thinking of all the companies.[140]

The need for a sizable class of new recruits each year is evident from some simple arithmetic. For any product to retain sales comparable to those of earlier years, new consumers must be brought in to replace consumers who leave the market, either due to death or other reasons. This need is magnified in the case of the cigarette industry because the industry loses 350,000 or more consumers per year to premature deaths caused by the product, a loss of life, and hence customers, for which there is no comparison among other products. Furthermore, since 1964 the industry has lost an average of one and a half million smokers each year to quitting. If the industry now loses from 1 to 1.5 million smokers to quitting and perhaps a million to death (an estimate of the number of smokers dying annually from both smoking-related and other causes), approximately 2 to 2.5 million people must become new smokers each year simply to keep constant the total number of smokers. With about 90 percent of beginning smokers being children and teenagers, this means that at least 5000 children and teens have to start smoking each and every day.

The need for new smokers does not imply that advertising alone is sufficiently effective to meet the need. But it does mean that the manufacturers have a powerful incentive to use all available vehicles to produce future sales among current nonsmokers. The obvious target must be children. The amount of advertising that the companies purchase in publications with large youthful readerships (e.g., $21 million in *Sports Illustrated* in 1980[141]) and the imagery of those ads strongly suggest that the industry does see market expansion potential in advertising.

Observation of smoking trends and levels in countries that do not permit cigarette advertising is a source of evidence to which both sides of the argument have appealed. Proponents of the industry perspective emphasize that in countries that do not permit cigarette advertising—primarily consisting of East European and other communist-bloc countries that have never permitted advertising—cigarette consumption is high and growing rapidly.[142] Smoking-and-health activists point to the case of Norway, in which a steady upward trend in per capita consumption was abruptly interrupted and reversed following the 1975 banning of cigarette advertising and introduction of several other antismoking measures.[143]

Each of these arguments lacks what scientists refer to as proper controls. The fact of increasing smoking in countries lacking advertising says nothing about whether advertising influences consumption. It simply indicates that advertising is not the only cause of smoking, a premise that no one would challenge. Indeed, growth in smoking during the years examined would have been expected in these countries, as smoking prevalence has been correlated with growing affluence in most countries until those countries enter a "post-industrial" phase. The appropriate question is how, if at all, the observed growth patterns would have been different if advertising had existed. If smoking would have increased faster or earlier, or achieved higher peak levels, then advertising would be assessed as influencing consumption. Only if the observed pattern were unaffected would one draw the conclusion that advertising did not influence consumption. The data needed to address this question do not exist.

The case of Norway is flawed too, in that the ad ban was not the only component of antismoking policy at the time. To the contrary, it was part of a package—certainly an important part—intended to discourage Norwegians from smoking. That the package worked seems evident; but the case does not offer definitive evidence that it was the ad ban that was principally or substantially responsible.

Formal Empirical Analysis. To the scientific mind, there is no substitute for the findings of a well-designed, carefully controlled scientific study. Unfortunately, the vagaries of reality often impinge upon the ability of scientists to construct and conduct the appropriate study. The appeal of formal analysis explains why so many participants in the advertising debate have turned to scientific studies to support their case. The realities of the analyses performed to date, however, limit the utility of their findings.

Two broad types of formal analysis address the issue of whether advertising affects cigarette consumption. One is the assessment of reactions to ads and their imagery, often then (or later) correlated with smoking behavior. Recall of cigarette brands and ad themes falls into this category, as do several other kinds of surveys. The subjects in such studies are often children, with the intent being to explore kids' interest in and response to cigarette ads.[144-147] One can also imagine experiments to study specific advertising-consumption questions. For example, one could observe smokers' cigarette consumption sitting in a waiting room with a Marlboro poster, compared with the behavior of similar smokers seated in an identical waiting room with a poster having a noncigarette theme. Such an experiment could test whether cigarette ads and imagery serve as cues stimulating greater consumption by smokers (personal communication with R. Davis, Centers for Disease Control).

Most of the studies that fall into this broad class of simulating or recalling advertising experiences and measuring responses to them provide evidence that cigarette ads are attention-getting and memorable, and that strength of interest correlates with smoking behavior, either current or future. The studies also show that children certainly are not "immune" to awareness of the ads, but rather are often quite attracted to them. Recall of cigarette brand names and ad themes is extraordinarily high. Yet despite these strong associations, the studies do not provide definitive evidence that there is a causal link between advertising and smoking.

On the opposite side of the issue, when children and adults are asked on surveys whether they think they are influenced to smoke by advertising, most respond negatively. The industry has used such findings as evidence of its position that advertising does not influence the basic decision of whether or not to smoke. The actual utility of this kind of questioning in evaluating the role of advertising is minimal, however. Conscious response to advertising is a poor index of actual response. One authority has referred to self-reports on the subject as "quite worthless."[148]

The second category of formal analysis is econometric (regression analysis) studies of the relationship between aggregate advertising expenditures and levels of cigarette consumption, over time and within a given country. To date, more than a dozen such studies have been performed and they have yielded mixed results. In one camp are a series of studies that find no statistically significant effect of ad expenditures on aggregate consumption.[149-152] In the other camp are studies that find statistically significant effects, particularly over the long run and when allowance is made for lagged responses to advertising campaigns.[153-157] Some scholars have identified a positive statistically significant relationship but have discounted its importance because it is so small.[83] It should be noted, however, that a small percentage response can represent a substantial absolute number of people, given a smoking population in excess of 50 million Americans.

The econometric studies are plagued by a series of technical problems, such as the modeling of lagged effects of advertising expenditures. Given the habitual nature of tobacco use and the investment nature of much advertising, one would not necessarily expect to find a substantial positive association between current-year advertising expenditures and current consumption, even if advertising ultimately did influence aggregate consumption. This is reflected in the findings of two studies that accounted for lagged effects and identified a statistically significant relationship between advertising and aggregate consumption over the long run.[153,155]

An additional technical problem is adequately controlling for changes in the environment in which cigarettes are sold and changes in the character of advertising. The environment has been in a state of flux for decades, with "health scares" and smoking policy activities constituting frequent "disruptions" that have evoked advertising responses. As several studies have shown, the basic character of cigarette advertising has changed frequently, and often radically, in apparent response to manufacturers' perceptions of public concern about the health issue.[111,114,119] Econometric studies, relying on gross measures such as aggregate advertising expenditures, cannot capture the qualitative aspects of various ad campaigns and may not adequately control for the adverse (i.e., antismoking) influences. Especially if some of the tobacco ad campaigns have been counterproductive, as some analysts believe,[111] treating all ad dollars as identical will obscure very distinct phenomena.

Complicating the reading of the econometric studies is the fact that the vast majority have not been designed to assess the consequences of an ad ban—a 100 percent decrease in advertising expenditures—yet they are being interpreted in the context of the ad ban debate. The technology of these regression analyses is such that estimated regression coefficient estimates can predict only the effects of *small* changes in the independent variables, unless certain very restrictive linearity conditions hold. While some of the findings in the literature have been read as indicating that advertising does not substantially influence the level of cigarette consumption, the only conclusion one can safely draw from these analyses is that *marginal* changes in the level of advertising have not significantly affected cigarette consumption *on the margin*.[158]

There is an additional theoretical reason that one might not expect to find a sizable statistically significant relationship between advertising and consumption: if manufacturers intend advertising to expand the overall market for their product *and* capture existing market share from competitors (or simply maintain their own market share), the rational level of advertising expenditure will exceed that which increases aggregate consumption. That is, *on the margin* the function of ad dollars will be to compete for existing market share, not to expand the overall market. Hence, regression analyses, examining marginal effects, would not be expected to demonstrate a strong correlation between advertising expenditures and aggregate consumption.

A handful of studies have attempted to measure the impacts of advertising bans directly. Schneider, Klein, and Murphy studied the 1971 broadcast ad ban in the U.S. and concluded that the ban *per se* was at most only mildly effective in reducing the demand for cigarettes. In its aggregate effects, they suggested, the ban actually may have worked to increase cigarette consumption by substantially reducing the costs of producing and distributing cigarettes, thereby lowering the price of cigarettes which, in turn, would increase demand.[159] Hamilton also saw the ad ban as a "Pyrrhic victory," although he attributed its failure to the associated loss of donated air time for antismoking messages under the Fairness Doctrine.[83]

Both of these studies offer limited insight into the long-run implications of the broadcast ad ban. Unless one assumes that the bulk of the impact of a ban would be experienced immediately, one must allow for the possibility of effects occurring well into the future, for example a reduction in the recruitment of successive generations of teenagers into the smoking population. This would be difficult to assess empirically, especially soon after the ban had taken effect. Hamilton's point about the relative effectiveness of pro-smoking advertising and antismoking messages similarly suffers from a short time horizon[82] and it depends on the coupling of pro- and anti-smoking advertising. There is no legal barrier to prohibiting tobacco ads and funding antismoking media education, although there is an obvious financing barrier to achieving the latter.

In another study, Hamilton also addressed the effect of broadcast ad bans on per capita cigarette consumption in several countries and did not find a significant relationship between the two variables.[160] Again, however, the analysis failed to control adequately for other potential influences, ranging from possible increases in other promotional activities to the passage of time sufficient to identify impacts.

In the attempts to evaluate the consumption impact of advertising at an empirical level, the principal issue of concern has largely escaped attention: does advertising specifically entice children and teenagers to smoke? Only one econometric study has addressed this question directly. Lewit and his colleagues examined teens' responses to the Fairness Doctrine and estimated the impact of the broadcast ad ban on the prevalence of smoking by teens. The researchers found that teens were quite responsive to the Fairness Doctrine messages, especially those that stressed the health hazards of smoking, a finding that runs contrary to the belief that teens do not respond to the health message. Further, Lewit *et al.* estimated that the ad ban reduced teen smoking prevalence by 0.6 percentage points from 1970 to 1974. Though not a substantial effect quantitatively, the analysis supports the notion that teen smoking does vary directly with the presence or absence of advertising and inversely with the presence or absence of counteradvertising.[90]

Direct Mechanisms: Concluding Observations. We should not be surprised that the evidence on the direct relationship between advertising and cigarette consumption does not yield a definitive answer to this analytically complex question. There is no technical statistical methodology available to address the fundamental question directly, and there is no obvious controlled experiment that would resolve the matter, simply because it is impossible to isolate a sample of the population from advertising over a long enough period to assess the implications.* Casual empiricism and lessons from logic and experience necessarily produce conflicting opinions, reflecting the political and emotional nature of the debate.

---

* It is possible, however, to design experiments to evaluate specific aspects of the matter. In the text we noted one example of this: a study of smokers' response to the visual stimulus of a cigarette ad in a waiting room. Such a study could determine whether the imagery of tobacco ads tends to increase consumption by smokers immediately. Even in this case, however, a finding that consumption was greater among smokers exposed to the ad would not necessarily prove that ads increase smokers' consumption. One could hypothesize that these same smokers would then smoke less over the next hour or two, having received a larger dose of nicotine while in the waiting room. This, too, is testable, however.

At the same time that no definitive answer is available, a summary review of the evidence does recommend a conclusion. The history and function of advertising, both for products in general and specifically for cigarettes, and the reality of the tobacco industry's behavior combine to strongly suggest that the people who should know best—the manufacturers and advertising experts—believe that advertising has influenced and can continue to affect the level of cigarette consumption. The empirical evidence points to the complexity of assessing precisely how and how much advertising affects consumption. Despite their limitations, the econometric studies support the thesis that additional (marginal) advertising expenditure in the aggregate has at best a small impact on increasing consumption. But these studies say nothing about the potential of targeted advertising (e.g., toward Hispanics), nor do they inform the debate over whether advertising *in toto* makes a difference, or whether the disappearance of advertising, through a legal ban, would make a difference; nor do they clarify the role of advertising in encouraging children to smoke.

Indirect Mechanisms

Ironically, the case linking advertising to smoking may be stronger for the indirect than the direct mechanisms, at least concerning the media coverage issue. The effects of advertising and promotional expenditures on the general social environment are numerous and diffuse. Although they are of great interest and importance, these influences have not been evaluated in a sufficiently rigorous manner. Thus we will focus on the influence of advertising on the media's coverage of smoking and health, and the consequent implications for public knowledge and smoking behavior. Taylor presents the best discussion of the social implications of the non-media institutional dependence on tobacco as a benefactor.[116]

In examining the evidence linking advertising to smoking through the vehicle of media censorship, one must address the several components of the logical chain: the relationship between media dependence on tobacco advertising and coverage of smoking and health; the relationship between media coverage and public understanding of the hazards of tobacco; and the relationship between understanding and smoking behavior. In Chapter 3 we discussed the last two of these. Thus here we focus on the evidence linking media coverage of smoking and health to dependence on advertising revenue. The implications of this evidence are then derived by integrating the evidence into the remaining components of the logical chain.

Cigarette Advertising Revenue and Media Coverage of Smoking. The evidence linking dependence on cigarette advertising revenue to suppression of coverage of smoking and health is abundant, if primarily anecdotal. While much of it has been developed recently,[120,161-165] some of the evidence dates back half a century.[113,166] Interest in the issue has arisen out of separate concerns with journalistic integrity and the health implications of suppression of coverage.

Distinguished journalists have addressed the relationship out of concern with the former. Bagdikian has referred to advertising-motivated suppression of coverage of smoking as the "most shameful money-induced" censorship of the American news media.[167] Writing in the journalism profession's watch-dog publication, the *Columbia Journalism Review*, Smith in 1978 characterized "[t]he records of national magazines that accept cigarette advertising . . . [as] dismal." He observed that *Newsweek* had failed to emphasize the central role of cigarette smoking in cancer in a 1976 cover story entitled "What Causes Cancer?" and he criticized *Time* for an attempt to discredit the growing protest against public smoking. With the exception of *Good Housekeeping*, women's magazines were identified as providing virtually no coverage of smoking and health.[168]

Among all the media, women's magazines stand out as the publications most influenced by cigarette ad revenues to restrict coverage of the hazards of tobacco. They are also the object of two of the four empirical studies that have examined the relationship between advertising and coverage.[169-172] In one of these, in 10 prominent women's magazines that carry cigarette advertisements, researchers found a total of eight feature articles from 1967 to 1979 that seriously discussed quitting or the dangers of smoking—less than one article per magazine for more than a decade. Four of the 10 magazines carried no antismoking articles in the entire 12-year period. By contrast, two prominent magazines that do not accept cigarette advertising, *Good Housekeeping* and *Seventeen*, ran 11 and five such articles, respectively. On average, the magazines that accept cigarette advertisements published from 12 to 63 times as many articles on each of nutrition, contraception, stress, and mental health as they did on the antismoking theme. *Good House-keeping* and *Seventeen* published three times as many articles on contraception as on smoking, two more articles on nutrition, and fewer on stress or mental health than on smoking.[171] A recent example of the lack of balance in the women's magazines that accept cigarette advertising is the May 1986 special issue of *Ms.* Entitled "The Beauty of Health," the issue had 15 articles under its theme, not one of which dealt with the leading cause of preventable illness and early death. The issue included four full-page cigarette ads, including the back cover.

In another empirical study, researchers examined coverage of smoking and health in a diverse group of prominent magazines recognized for their coverage of health matters in general. Publications selected for the study included a minimum of 60 articles on health topics during the years 1965 to 1981. The percentage of health articles devoted to smoking was compared to the percentage of advertising revenues derived from cigarette ads. Only four of the magazines devoted as many as one out of 10 of their health-related articles to "the chief, single, avoidable cause of death in our society and the most important public health issue of our time."[1] Of these four, the top three—*Reader's Digest, Good Housekeeping*, and *Prevention*—do not accept cigarette advertising. The proportion of health articles that dealt with smoking in those magazines was 34.4 percent, 22.1 percent, and 15.4 percent, respectively. Of the magazines that accept tobacco advertising, the only magazine to devote more than one of 10 health articles to smoking (11.7 percent) was *Vogue*; at 5.1 percent of total revenues, its cigarette advertisement share of advertising income was the lowest of the remaining magazines. The percentage of advertising revenues from cigarettes in other magazines ranged from 7.1 percent to 17.2 percent, with the percentage of health articles discussing smoking varying from 7.4 percent to none (including *Ms.* and *Redbook* among the latter). There was no substantial correlation between the volume of advertisements and smoking coverage within this group of magazines, but the contrast between the magazines that accept cigarette advertisements and those that do not was striking.[169] (See Table 8.)

The handful of correlational studies, including a new one by the American Council on Science and Health,[172] certainly supports the contention that dependence on cigarette advertising revenues influences magazines' editorial policy regarding tobacco. One could

Table 8. Cigarette Ad Revenues and Coverage of Smoking and Health, Selected Magazines[a]

Magazine	Years surveyed	% Health articles discussing smoking	Cig. ad revenue as % of total ad revenue
Reader's Digest	1965–81	34.4	0
Good Housekeeping	1965–81	22.1	0
Prevention	1967–78	15.4	0
Vogue	1965–81	11.7	5.1
U.S. News & World Report	1965–81	7.4	14.6
Ladies' Home Journal	1968–81	7.1	16.3
Time	1965–81	6.9	17.2
Harper's Bazaar	1968–81	4.5	7.1
McCall's	1969–80	4.5	15.1
Newsweek	1969–81	2.9	15.8
Cosmopolitan	1971–81	2.3	9.4
Mademoiselle	1966–81	1.9	7.3
Ms.	1972–81	0	14.8
Redbook	1970–81	0	16.1

Note:
[a] Magazines listed included a minimum of 60 health-related articles in the years surveyed.

Source:
Dale, pp. 8–9.

argue, however, that the mechanism of causality is the opposite, at least in part; that is, it is possible that publications that have editors or publishers who have strong antismoking sentiments, and perhaps a desire to campaign in their publications to discourage smoking, choose not to accept cigarette advertising. Thus, rather than advertising revenues impeding coverage, magazines not accepting cigarette advertising might provide "excess" coverage, the result of the editors' or publishers' excessive zeal. By this logic, the norm of acceptance of cigarette advertising and limited coverage of smoking and health might reflect balanced coverage. While the percentages of health articles in magazines accepting cigarette ads fall dramatically short of the relative health importance of smoking, the deficit could be attributed to such factors as the widespread belief that everyone knows that smoking is dangerous and the perception that smoking is old news, stale news.[173]

The anecdotal evidence on the influence of ad revenues limits the plausibility of this argument. Dozens of writers, editors, and publishers have described instances of censorship on coverage of tobacco attributed directly to publications' fears of alienating cigarette advertisers. The cases apply to a wide spectrum of magazines and even newspapers, although to a lesser extent.

Numerous examples of censorship in women's magazines have been reported by health writers asked to prepare articles for the magazines. The censorship has been either complete—removal from an article of references to smoking or refusal to publish an article because of its emphasis on smoking—or partial. As an example of complete censorship, the American Council on Science and Health reports that *Harper's Bazaar* rejected a science writer's article entitled "Protect Your Man from Cancer" after it was commissioned and paid for, because, according to the editor, "it focused too much on tobacco," and "the magazine is running three full-page, color ads [for tobacco] this month."[169] Television investigative reporter John Stossel has stated on the show, *20/20*, "The publisher [of *Family Circle*] denies that cigarette articles are censored, yet a few years ago, the magazine asked me to write an article and said, 'Don't write about cigarettes. It might offend advertisers.' "[174]

Partial censorship has taken such forms as "softening" references to smoking—qualifying them—for example, by an editor's inserting the adjective "heavy" into a statement that smoking is dangerous (i.e., "heavy smoking is dangerous"), and moving references to the hazards of tobacco to the end of lengthy articles, when the author had placed them at the beginning. Whelan and her colleagues have reported several examples of this kind.[17,171] Similarly, Okie, a physician who writes a health column for *Cosmopolitan*, says that smoking is the one subject (except occasionally for alcohol abuse) for which "softening" editing occurs regularly. Okie is convinced that this type of editing is a response to editors' concerns about alienating tobacco advertisers (personal communication, March 18, 1986). Helen Gurley Brown, the publisher of *Cosmopolitan*, has essentially acknowledged this in the case of her magazine. In an article in the *Washington Post*, she is quoted as saying, "Having come from the advertising world myself, I think, 'Who needs somebody you're paying millions of dollars a year to come back and bite you on the ankle?' "[120]

Brown's response is unusually candid. Several writers and reporters have been told by editors and publishers, off the record, that the censorship issue is real and occurs with regularity. Few of these editors and publishers are willing to say this on the record, however. And when some have been asked about the issue on the record, they have denied that censorship exists, despite the fact that they had confirmed it in earlier off-the-record discussions.

The author of an article on the censorship issue, eventually published in the *Washington Monthly*, alleges that this is what happened in the case of his article, originally prepared for the *New Republic*.[162,163]

Much of the purported influence of cigarette advertising appears to take the form of media self-censorship, reflecting publishers' perceptions that substantial revenues will be lost if a publication openly addresses the issue of smoking and health. Illustrative of the fear some publishers feel is the example of a reporter who was fired in 1982, after writing a preview of the Kool Jazz Festival in which he labeled a disease caused by smoking as "un-Kool" and noted that Duke Ellington had died from lung cancer. According to the reporter, "The publisher . . . called me in to his office [the next day] and he said, 'If we have to fly to Louisville, Kentucky, and crawl on our bended knees and beg the cigarette company not to take their ads out of our newspaper, we'll do that.' And then he told me, 'You're fired.' " When questioned about the characterization of the situation, the publisher said, simply, "True."[174]

The avoidance of discussion of smoking is dramatic, if not necessarily obvious (due to its absence), in the obituaries published by both newspapers and magazines. Typically, the victim of a smoking-related death is described as succumbing following "a long illness"; or the disease may be labelled as "cancer", but rarely "lung cancer." Even when cancer or lung cancer is indicated as the cause, it is extremely rare to see the victim's smoking status referenced. In part, one might assume that this occurs out of respect for the family of the deceased. This is what the *New York Times* informed Elizabeth Whelan when she inquired why the story on the death of a prominent New York City politician in his middle 50s had not mentioned that he was a heavy smoker and had died of lung cancer. Whelan questioned this motivation when she noted that the death announcement placed by the family, at the bottom of the same page as the story, requested that donations be sent to the Sloan-Kettering Memorial Cancer Center for lung cancer research (personal communication, August 15, 1986). Families' wishes certainly should be respected; and no one would argue that obituaries should be the forum for a crusade against smoking. Nevertheless, the virtually complete failure of publications to identify decedents' smoking status implies the loss of a potentially powerful educational tool regarding smoking and health.

The censorship phenomenon appears to extend to other tobacco products, in addition to cigarettes. Recently, the author of an article on athletes' giving up smokeless tobacco was told by a baseball writer of *Sports Illustrated* that the magazine's management might perceive a "conflict of interest" in publishing an article that was negative on a product advertised in the magazine. Despite favorable reviews by the baseball writer and a senior editor, the article was turned down.[175]

It has been suggested that it is standard practice for major advertisers to be alerted in advance about stories that could be detrimental to their business; until the early 1980s, R.J. Reynolds reportedly requested such notification routinely.[176] Illustrative of the potential consequence of this policy is the June 6, 1983, issue of *Newsweek*. That issue included a four and one-half page article on the nonsmokers' rights movement, and it carried no advertisements for cigarettes. With cigarette ads typically bringing in up to $1 million per issue in *Newsweek*, the decision to publish the article appears to have been an expensive one. *Newsweek* claims that its tobacco advertisers learned of the intended article as a result of calls for information from reporters and requested that their advertisements be moved to later issues.[177] To corroborate this claim, we reviewed the numbers and distribution of ads in the issues preceding and following the June 6 issue for three months in each direction, and we compared them with the ads in the same months for 1982 and 1984. We could find no pattern of ads that would be consistent with *Newsweek*'s claim.

Another example of the relation between advertising and coverage is the 1978 and 1979 cancellation by three tobacco companies of all their cigarette advertisements in *Mother Jones*, after publication of two articles on tobacco. An editor of *Mother Jones* said that the companies "made it clear that *Mother Jones* would never get cigarette advertising again." Loss of these advertisements caused the magazine "severe problems from the considerable lost revenue."[171]

The experiences of *Newsweek* and *Mother Jones* illustrate that although no publication is exempt from the editorial pressure associated with cigarette advertising, smaller publications may be particularly vulnerable. A major national publication may have enough market power to afford an occasional article or commentary on the hazards of smoking. The publication's profits may permit the one-time loss of revenue, to whatever extent it occurs, and the size of its readership makes the cancellation of cigarette advertisements an unlikely punishment. For the smaller publica-tions, however, economic viability is typically marginal, adding importance to all advertising revenue, and circulation is insufficient to ensure the cigarette companies' allegiance.

While the broadcast media have provided a few excellent programs on tobacco and health issues in recent years, studies of broadcast programming have found little coverage, particularly in the years preceding the 1971 ban on cigarette advertising in broadcasting. One study of television coverage did not find a single documentary on smoking from 1938 through 1955, the era in which the first solid scientific research was being published and discussed in the scientific community. The study also showed that television stations completely ignored three major smoking-and-health news events in 1960.[178] On a public television panel, Howard K. Smith bemoaned the fact that a 1965 CBS documentary on smoking and health had created the impression of balance between the opinions of medical professionals, "who had every reason to be objective," and representatives of the tobacco industry, "who have no reason to be objective." "The public was left with a blurred impression that the truth [about the role of smoking in cancer] lay between [the two sides] whereas . . . we have everything but a signed confession from a cigarette that smoking has a causal relation to cancer."[167]

Censorship is found in other media as well. According to Whelan, thousands of dollars raised to place antismoking messages on billboards were rejected by a billboard company "because it didn't want to alienate its tobacco clients."[179]

Critics of the media's coverage of smoking and health emphasize the exemplary coverage of a few publications that do not accept cigarette advertising. Preeminent among these is *Reader's Digest*. Even the *Digest*, however, has experienced the monetary influence of the tobacco industry. Because of the magazine's vigorous coverage of smoking and health, it has been reported, the American Tobacco Company asked the *Digest*'s advertising agency to drop its account with the magazine. The account was worth $1.3 million, but the American Tobacco Company's account with the same agency was worth $22 million. The wishes of the tobacco company were respected.[167]

The influence of cigarette advertising extends not only to editorial policy but also to advertising policy. Some publishers have re-portedly rejected advertising solely because it had an antismoking message. For example, the president of World Wide Media, Grace Reinbold, reported difficulties in placing advertisements for antismoking clinics. Of 36 national magazines contacted by Reinbold, "22 . . . responded with an absolute 'no' to anti-tobacco advertising but would not state an explicit reason." *Psychology Today* would not accept any advertising with an antismoking theme, telling Reinbold, "we have a lot of money that comes in from tobacco companies, and frankly, we don't want to offend our tobacco advertisers." *Cosmopolitan* also refused to accept the advertisements, noting that "we get 200 pages of cigarette advertising . . . [A]m I going to jeopardize $5 or $10 million worth of business?" Three magazines were willing to accept Reinbold's advertisements.[174,180]

The potential reach of the influence of tobacco company advertising extends to the threat of loss of *non-tobacco* product advertising for products sold by the cigarette-manufacturing conglomerates. Given tobacco company ownership of consumer products companies such as Nabisco and General Foods, the potential for economic intimidation of virtually any publication is self-evident. As a dramatic example, given its record of coverage of smoking, the *Reader's Digest* has been reported to have recently rejected a proposal from the American Heart Association to publish an advertising supplement on heart disease because the supplement would have discussed the role of smoking. According to a Heart Association memo, the editors of the *Digest* "voiced concern that they would not be able to find sponsors because their major advertisers are food companies now owned by tobacco companies."[179] Obviously, such intimidation can extend to the broadcast media as well. Recently, for example, an antismoking public service announcement was turned down by a New York City radio station reluctantly but explicitly due to fear of loss of nontobacco ad revenues from the tobacco conglomerates.[181]

If there is such a thing as a "paragon of virtue" in journalism, many people think that it is the *New York Times*. Indeed, the *Times* deserves credit for having insisted on health warnings on cigarette ads before they were legally required and for occasionally providing excellent coverage of smoking-and-health issues. Nevertheless, the *Times'* record with regard to tobacco is not unblemished. Emblematic is the years-long correspondence that Dr. George Gitlitz, a New York State vascular surgeon, carried on with the *Times* concerning the paper's acceptance of cigarette ads.

He wrote numerous letters, several intended as letters-to-the-editor, yet not one was ever published. Responses to the others, when they were offered, were uninformative. The correspondence, much of it published in 1983 in the *New York State Journal of Medicine*, makes for fascinating, telling reading.[182] Gitlitz finally succeeded in getting the *Times* to agree to publish an op ed column by him on the subject of cigarette advertising and journalistic responsibility. But the *Times* required Gitlitz to "depersonalize" the article by changing references to the *Times'* responsibility to refer to the responsibility of newspapers in general.[183]

The issue of the media's coverage of smoking and health and its relation to dependence on advertising revenues was accented in recent years by two episodes in which major medical associations apparently went along with major publications' insistence to downplay or ignore smoking as a health hazard. In both instances, the associations were responsible for writing special supplements on personal health care, supplements that purported to tell readers what they could do to improve and preserve their own health. Mentioned in Chapter 3, these episodes warrant description here both because they add to the evidence that the media restrict discussion of smoking and because they illustrate that even major medical organizations have capitulated to pressure to avoid the topic.

The first supplement was prepared by the American Medical Association and published in *Newsweek* on November 7, 1983. "This special supplement," the introduction said, "offers easily understandable information on good health from the most knowledgeable and dependable source available: the medical profession itself." The supplement promised to discuss "the most important things" related to health and devoted full pages among its 16 pages of text to detailed advice on diet, exercise, weight control, and stress. Although the Surgeon General considers smoking the most important public health issue of our time, the AMA-*Newsweek* supplement mentioned cigarettes in only four sentences, none of which explicitly identified smoking as a health hazard. The same issue of *Newsweek* contained 12 pages of cigarette advertisements, worth close to $1 million in revenues.

In response to an inquiry, a spokesperson for *Newsweek* said, "we naturally share concerns regarding smoking . . . but hope that you understand that there is just not enough space sometimes to do justice to all the subjects involved."[184] The executive director of the AMA explained that "[s]ince smoking . . . and [its] effect on health are actually quite complex subjects for people to accept, and since most people need counseling and help to deal with them, it was thought that these subjects are best discussed with a physician to allow for the greatest interaction between the person with the habit . . . and the person who can best explain and advise on a proper course of action."[185] Thus, in 16 pages of text on "the most important things" one could do to improve one's health, *Newsweek* claimed it "just [didn't have] enough space" to discuss the leading cause of premature death and avoidable illness. The AMA suggested that the health effects of smoking are more complex for people to understand than the less well-established health effects of moderate overweight, stress, and a sedentary life style. Furthermore, the AMA implied that people are better prepared to deal by themselves with sustained weight reduction, for example, than with quitting smoking. Yet an estimated 95 percent of the 34 million people who have permanently quit smoking have done so on their own, while sustained weight loss, on one's own or through an organized program, is a relative rarity.

An alternative explanation for the omission of discussion of smoking in the supplement is found in a letter from the science news editor of the AMA to a physician in the state of Washington: "[The AMA's] intention, expressed and argued, was to have a much stronger statement . . . [about] smoking. *Newsweek* resisted any mention of cigarettes . . . "[186] As the supplement shows, the AMA went along with *Newsweek*'s insistence.

Less than a year later, on October 8, 1984, *Time* magazine published a similar supplement, produced by the American Academy of Family Physicians. The text of this supplement contained absolutely no references to smoking and a brief health quiz included questions about smoking behavior that had been sufficiently distorted as to give the appearance that "moderate" smoking was "okay". In an unpublished letter to the editor of *Time*, the chairman of the board of the Academy expressed "disappointment that editors of the supplement chose to edit out narrative references to the health hazards involved in smoking cigarettes . . . in the final copy."[187] The implicit suggestion of the letter was that the removal of references to smoking was accomplished without the knowledge of the Academy. More recently, however, the Academy acknowledged that it had been aware of *Time*'s progressive elimination of material on tobacco in successive drafts and, like the AMA in the

80

Newsweek case, had chosen to go along with the deletions rather than forego the supplement altogether.[120] The October 8 issue of *Time* contained eight pages of cigarette ads.

The medical societies', and the magazines', avoidance of the subject of the hazards of smoking ultimately may contribute to the health toll of smoking. Certainly the message conveyed to the public by the supplements is that the nation's leading medical authorities do not consider the hazards of smoking to rival those of moderate overweight, stress, or a sedentary life style. This is precisely the kind of coverage that can contribute to the public's gross underestimation of the dangers of smoking, discussed in Chapter 3. The potential impact is illustrated by the report of the executive director of a consumer health organization that smokers are using the supplements to justify their continued smoking because "even the AMA doesn't think cigarettes are worth mentioning."[188]

The first AMA/*Newsweek* supplement created substantial professional criticism of the AMA.[96] Such criticism may have contributed to the AMA's decision to include a brief but strong statement on the hazards of smoking in a second *Newsweek* supplement, published October 29, 1984. The five paragraphs on smoking constituted only four percent of the entire text of the supplement. Nevertheless, it is interesting to note that that issue of *Newsweek* contained only four pages of cigarette advertisements.

On September 9, 1985, *Newsweek* published its third AMA supplement on personal health care. Like the first supplement, this one virtually ignored smoking. In discussing the prevention of cancer, the text dedicated 11 paragraphs to breast cancer, which it erroneously identified as the leading cause of cancer death in women, and six of these paragraphs discussed breast self-examination. In startling contrast, lung cancer—which in 1985 surpassed breast cancer as the leading cancer killer of women—received mention in only one paragraph, in which the AMA noted that "lung cancer . . . [is] linked to . . . cigarette smoking." The supplement offered no advice to smokers as to resources to help them to quit; nor did it address the primary prevention of smoking.

The American Academy of Family Physicians reportedly asked *Time* to permit the Academy to prepare a second supplement, but with the understanding that the Academy would retain editorial control of the text. *Time* refused to agree to this constraint and the Academy decided not to prepare another supplement for *Time*.[95]

If the media have avoided the bad news about smoking, they have shown no reluctance in dealing with the "good news." Above we noted that the obituaries of victims of smoking-related diseases rarely mention the decedent's smoking status. Yet a few years ago, when comedian Andy Kaufmann died at an early age of lung cancer, the nation's newspapers made a significant news story out of the fact that Kaufmann was a "health nut" and lifelong nonsmoker. The coverage undoubtedly reinforced the public's substantial underestimation of the importance of smoking in lung cancer.

A second dramatic illustration of an apparent enthusiasm for promoting the "good news" side of the tobacco story was *Cosmopolitan*'s recent (January 1986) article on smoking and health. The magazine's first article on this subject in many years, the story reported the findings of a single scientific study suggesting that heavy smokers have a lower rate of endometrial cancer than nonsmokers, and noting that quitters' risk of endometrial cancer approached that of never-smokers a few years after quitting. While the story mentioned the "downside" to smoking and cancer, the headline and emphasis of the story could reassure the smoking reader that the cancer risks and benefits of smoking roughly "balance out." *Cosmopolitan* is regarded by the American Council on Science and Health as providing the worst coverage of tobacco of all the major women's magazines.[172]

Evidence such as that presented here strongly suggests that the public is fed a media diet deficient in accurate news, comment, and commercial promotion relating to the adverse consequences of smoking. Bagdikian has observed that "medical evidence on tobacco and disease has been treated differently from any other information on carriers of disease that do not advertise." In support of this contention, he noted that "In 1980 . . . there were still more stories in the daily press about the cause of influenza, polio, and tuberculosis than about the cause of one of every seven deaths in the United States."[167]

Implications of Suppression of Media Coverage. The chain connecting cigarette advertising revenues to smoking behavior, and ultimately to health effects, has several links, each firmly in place. That some of the media, especially magazines, are highly dependent on cigarette advertising revenues is clear from a simple examination of the dollar volume of such revenues and their percentage contribution to the total advertising revenues of those media. That that financial dependency translates into media self-censorship on the subject of tobacco and health seems obvious from the wealth of anecdotal evidence and the direct testimony of the involved actors. While the case relies on anecdotes and testimony, their sheer quantity and power together lead to the clear conclusion that the media's coverage of tobacco is affected by dependence on tobacco ad revenues. The public, one must conclude, is receiving substantially less (and less accurate) information on and editorial discussion of the hazards of tobacco than it would be were tobacco merely an agent of disease that did not advertise.

The next link in the chain follows logically and is supported by a wealth of survey evidence: the public's knowledge of and attitude toward tobacco have been affected significantly by what coverage the media have afforded the subject. Suppression of coverage means that the public's knowledge base is less than it would be had coverage reflected the inherent newsworthiness of the topic. Suppression of coverage undoubtedly contributes to the surprising superficiality of the public's understanding, described in Chapter 3.

That increased knowledge of tobacco's hazards has altered smoking behavior is well-established by a myriad of behavioral changes all consistent with the knowledge change that has occurred. Fewer people are smoking today than would be the case had the hazards of smoking never been studied and brought to the public's attention; among smokers, there is a strong tendency to adopt smoking behaviors that are perceived to be less hazardous (e.g., low t/n cigarettes). Nevertheless, the "residual" smoking population includes 56 million members, almost a quarter of the American public, including children. On average, they smoke a pack and a half per day, 11,000 cigarettes per year. About 350,000 of them will die each year as the result of their habits. Hundreds of thousands of others will suffer as the result of smoking-related illness and disability.

The bottom line is that the media's yielding to the pressure of tobacco ad dollars is likely responsible for thousands, perhaps millions, of Americans continuing to smoke who would not be doing so had the media simply covered tobacco as they would any other comparably important cause of disease that was not the object of a multi-billion dollar advertising campaign. The logical conclusion is a strong one, yet it is inescapable: people have died and will die as the result of the media's failure to accord tobacco and health the coverage that is warranted by the inherent interest and importance of the subject.

The potential significance of this conclusion is suggested by the finding that, as the result of their antismoking campaign-induced decisions to quit smoking or not to start, over 200,000 Americans did *not* die prematurely in the first 15 years following the Surgeon General's report.[189] While this accomplishment ranks high among the public health accomplishments of the century, almost four million other Americans *did* die of smoking-related diseases during the same years. It can only be left to conjecture as to how many of those four million people would not have died prematurely, how many would be alive today, if the media had simply done their job.

Summary and Conclusion

To the tobacco industry and its allies in the media and the field of advertising, cigarette advertising serves merely to allocate slices of a market pie of fixed size to the various cigarette companies. To members of the public health community, advertising and promotion are significant weapons in a tobacco industry arsenal dedicated to recruiting new smokers.

The evidence suggests that attributing a singular or exclusive role to advertising and promotion is inappropriate. The brand-share function is undoubtedly a major one. Yet the logical and empirical case for concluding that advertising and promotion encourage cigarette consumption, including initiation of the habit, substantially dominates the case against this proposition. The formal analytical evidence on the direct effects of advertising leaves room for uncertainty, but the preponderance of evidence of all types supports the existence of a relationship between promotion and cigarette consumption. The evidence on the indirect effects—the suppression and distortion of media coverage of tobacco, and the consequent impact on the public's knowledge and smoking behavior—leaves little room for doubt.

CHAPTER 6

POLICY ALTERNATIVES

The idea of restricting or regulating promotion of tobacco products is not new. Smoking itself was illegal in many states early in the century.[17] In the latter half of the century, federal regulation has included the requirement that cigarette packs and ads carry a health warning label and advertising has been banned from the broadcast media. At the state and local level, a variety of other promotional activities have been prohibited, such as free distribution of product samples on a city's streets. Internationally, dozens of countries impose restrictions on cigarette advertising, including the complete banning of cigarette ads.[144,190]

Whether or not tobacco promotion warrants further remedial action in the United States—perhaps a philosophical as much as factual question—powerful social voices have raised the matter with a forcefulness that has not been experienced for a decade and a half. Recent calls for a ban on tobacco promotion by major health organizations have commanded a position for the question on the national health policy agenda. The ban proposal—the most restrictive and hence most dramatic of several alternatives—is center stage at present, but alternative policy measures are also receiving attention.

The present chapter discusses the ban and outlines the nature of alternative policy measures, identifying the major issues that each raises. Evaluation of the potential effectiveness of these measures is limited both by the availability of relevant objective evidence and by the imprecise articulation of the purpose of the measures. Some proponents of restrictions on advertising and promotion base their advocacy on the expectation that restrictions would result in substantial decreases in tobacco use. Others might wish to alter a perceived imbalance in the public's exposure to pro- and anti-tobacco information. Still others may simply seek the elimination of the inconsistency of the legal glamorization of tobacco use and governmental labeling of tobacco as the nation's most important public health problem.

Banning Promotion of Tobacco Products

The notion of a comprehensive prohibition of all forms of promotion of all tobacco products is fairly new in the United

States. Calls by major health organizations for the elimination of cigarette advertising date back almost two decades—in 1967, the American Cancer Society urged voluntary cessation of advertising[191]—but the new campaign is unique in its intensity and breadth. The more timid call for voluntary restrictions is gone; all recent proposals have called for federal legislation. Reflecting a growing awareness of the diversity of promotional techniques, and the steady growth in the nonadvertising share of the tobacco companies' promotional budgets, proposals now cover all forms of promotion and not simply advertising. Reflecting rapid diffusion of the smokeless tobacco habit among teenage boys, and the associated advertising and promotion campaign, proposals cover all forms of tobacco use. In the space of less than half a year, from late 1985 to early 1986, three of the nation's most influential health organizations—the American Heart Association, American Medical Association, and American Cancer Society—issued calls for the abolition of tobacco advertising and promotion. In so doing, they joined forces with numerous other prominent national and international health organizations that have supported bans covering the spectrum from cigarette advertising alone to all forms of promotion of all tobacco products.*

The call for a ban raises issues ranging from the philosophical to the purely pragmatic. The most visible and fundamental is the question of free speech, or more specifically in this instance commercial free speech, the right of the producers of a legal product to advertise and the right of consumers to have access through ads to information on legal products.

At the opposite end of the spectrum, one of the most significant pragmatic issues is that withdrawal of hundreds of millions of dollars of cigarette advertising revenues might jeopardize the

---

* The Board of Directors of the nation's other major voluntary health organization, the American Lung Association, passed a resolution "encourag[ing] the cessation" of tobacco advertising and promotion in December 1983. The resolution did not state whether "encouragement" referred to voluntary or legal means. In December 1985, however, the Board commended the AMA for joining the ALA in the effort to eliminate tobacco promotion. This was followed in short order (May 1986) by a resolution describing detailed steps to achieve the elimination.[192] Other health organizations that have called for bans, many within the year preceding the announcements by the AHA, AMA, and ACS, include the American Academy of Pediatrics, American Academy of Family Physicians, American College of Emergency Physicians, National Advisory Council on Drug Abuse, British Medical Society, Canadian Medical Association, and World Health Organization.

existence of some publications and the quality of others. Similarly, the availability of concerts, art exhibits, and sports events might be diminished by loss of tobacco sponsorship, especially in the short run. Also at issue are such questions as what difference a ban would make in Americans' smoking behavior—the focus of much of the preceding discussion—and whether less restrictive policies might achieve desired effects while proving less threatening to First Amendment freedoms. An important pragmatic question is whether a ban-produced decrease in tobacco company costs would lead to product price reductions that, in turn, would increase the demand for tobacco products; and if so, how such demand increases would compare with possible decreases reflecting the elimination of advertising and promotion.

The free speech issue is the most fundamental philosophical question and the most obvious grounds for developing an impressive coalition in opposition to a ban. While the principle of free speech deserves the widest and broadest protection, several qualifications apply in this instance. First, does commercial free speech differ from political, religious, and other types of free speech? Court decisions clearly draw distinctions between these, but different legal scholars have arrived at different conclusions as to the applicability of the body of case law to the question of the ban. Several leading experts, including independent consultants and a government attorney, have concluded that a ban would not violate First Amendment protections,[193-195] but others believe that it would.[196,197] A recent Supreme Court case lends credence to the position that a ban would be found constitutional. On July 1, 1986, the Court ruled that Puerto Rico could prohibit advertising of casino gambling, despite the legality of the activity. Of particular interest, the majority opinion suggested that states could ban or restrict advertising "of products or activities deemed harmful, such as cigarettes, alcoholic beverages, and prostitution."[198] Despite this decision—representing a 5-4 split among the justices—the diversity of opinion and the complexity of the issues seem certain to occasion a court battle should Congress legislate a ban.

In part, the issue revolves around a pragmatic question: could the desired social effect be accomplished by less restrictive regulatory measures? Both legal theory and case law suggest that commercial speech can be restricted to achieve a compelling (and competing) social goal, such as preservation of the public's health, but the law seems to call for the least infringement upon commercial free speech necessary to attain the goal. Ban proponents argue that anything short of a complete ban would fail to eliminate the negative health consequences they perceive to derive from tobacco advertising and promotion. Opponents of a ban, including some health professionals who find tobacco promotion distasteful, question whether even a complete ban would significantly affect tobacco consumption. In this context, empirical analysis of the effects of promotion becomes relevant; and the difficulties of such analysis, discussed above, are highlighted.

The commercial free speech argument is muted conceptually, if not necessarily legally, by the fact that free speech for tobacco advertisers appears to translate into restricted speech for the media recipients of tobacco ad expenditures, as discussed in the preceding chapter. If the journalism profession could resolve this issue, this concern might diminish in importance. But the economics of tobacco advertising seem so compelling as to make universal voluntary elimination of the problem appear essentially unattainable. If this is true, then the appropriate framing of the issue may be the choice between competing restrictions on genuinely free speech, with the media's freedom restricted at present and the tobacco industry's freedom restricted in the event of a ban.*

The notion that tobacco advertising should be legal because tobacco products are legal products is the fundamental rallying cry of ban opponents. Its apparent appeal is diminished, however, when one considers the nature of the legality of tobacco products. First, use of tobacco products is *not* universally legal. Sale to children is illegal in over three-quarters of the states (with minimum purchase ages varying). In other instances in which products are not legally available to minors, advertising has been restricted, often severely and occasionally completely. A notable example is the wares available in "adult book stores."

Second, the legality of tobacco products stems from historical accident and deliberate circumvention of the nation's legal and regulatory apparatus intended to deal with hazardous substances. The historical accident is that tobacco use diffused widely before

---

* For reasons discussed above, banning tobacco ads would not eliminate the advertising revenue pressure for the media to downplay coverage of tobacco issues; the tobacco companies are now among the leading producers, and advertisers, of nontobacco consumer products. A ban, however, would almost certainly diminish the perceived pressure to avoid coverage of tobacco and health. This in turn would likely increase such coverage.

the hazards of tobacco were well understood. Apart from judging its philosophical merits, banning tobacco products today would be wholly impractical, as it would make criminals out of more than 50 million law-abiding citizens who are physiologically and psychologically dependent on their tobacco products.

Tobacco products are legal today solely because they have been specifically exempted, by legislation or administrative decision, from the regulatory authority of numerous federal agencies mandated to protect the public from hazardous products. In several instances, federal law clearly would require the banning of tobacco product sales were it not for the explicit exemption of these products. For example, federal legislation specifically precludes the Consumer Products Safety Commission from considering the safety of cigarettes, despite the fact that cigarettes are responsible for more deaths than the combination of all of the other products that have come under the Commission's purview. As a second example, the Food and Drug Administration has repeatedly chosen not to evaluate the safety of tobacco products, claiming that they are neither food nor medication. Yet the makers of a nicotine-based chewing gum, an aid to smoking cessation, secured FDA approval before marketing their product, and it is available only with a doctor's prescription. As a further irony, the stringent Delaney clause requires that food additives found to cause cancer in laboratory animals must be removed from the market. Yet the nation's most significant source of cancer death escapes coverage. With tobacco products' legality predicated on such exceptional grounds, ban advocates perceive an exception to the legal-to-sell, legal-to-advertise principle as readily justifiable.

Support for the legal-to-sell, legal-to-advertise principle has been echoed by a number of interested parties, ranging from the tobacco industry, to associations of advertisers, to the media, to the American Civil Liberties Union. While the theme is invariably couched in terms of basic principles, several adherents have an obvious practical economic interest in the outcome of the ban debate. In the case of the tobacco industry, the relative importance of principle and pragmatic economic considerations is suggested by the experience of the late 1960s, when the industry worked quietly to encourage the broadcast media ad ban in order to eliminate the Fairness Doctrine antismoking messages.[115]

Pragmatic considerations head the list of concerns of several interest groups. The notion that removal of tobacco advertising would jeopardize the economic viability of some publications has some basis in fact, although the likely extent of this phenomenon has been exaggerated. While some economically marginal publications might be forced out of business, the vast majority probably would adjust with relative ease. This was the experience of the broadcast media following the 1971 ban, despite dire predictions to the contrary. A similar assessment applies to cultural activities and sporting events, with the viability of selected events jeopardized in the short run.

A pragmatic and philosophical concern is that the banning of tobacco advertising might generalize to other products, such as alcoholic beverages, foods high in cholesterol or salt, automobiles, and so on. To this idea, ban advocates respond by noting that the same concern was raised at the time of the cigarette broadcast ad ban and the fears proved to be wholly unwarranted. Ban advocates also point to the quantitative and even qualitative uniqueness of the problem of tobacco use. Tobacco products, they argue, constitute the only significant legal consumer products that are harmful when used as intended. Furthermore, the magnitude of the harm associated with this product is unprecedented and has no parallels today. And most smokers become addicted before they reach the age of legal accountability.

This last point underlies one of the proponents' strongest arguments for a ban on promotion of tobacco products. The cigarette manufacturers claim that they do not want children to smoke. A wide variety of evidence, and simple logic, indicates that the industry cannot genuinely hold this position. Tobacco experimentation typically begins in the early teens, and the habit of regular cigarette smoking is usually established today by the mid-teens; rarely does smoking begin in adulthood. Further, it is the addictiveness of tobacco that sustains much of its use. Without children adopting tobacco habits, ban advocates conclude, tobacco use would diminish dramatically. Thus it is essential for the survival of the industry that children be attracted to tobacco, and it appears to ban proponents to be no accident that many tobacco promotions portray role models the young aspire to emulate.

That the public might be offended by tobacco companies using advertising to encourage tobacco use by children is emphasized by the very fact that the tobacco companies are so vehement in their protestations that they do not advertise to children. The appropriate question, then, is how society can assure that tobacco use is engaged in only by the truly knowledgeable, consenting adult. Discouraging the initiation of use in the impressionable teenage years would seem to be essential to this. To proponents of a promotion ban, eliminating the seductive imagery of tobacco advertising is vital to discouraging initiation of smoking and smokeless tobacco use by teenagers. Prohibiting tobacco advertising would have this effect, at least in the print media. Restricting sponsorship of sports events could help to dispel the association between tobacco and athletics.

The fundamental question remains, however, as to whether or not, and how much, advertising and promotion entice children to use tobacco products. The conventional wisdom of the health community—that promotion does encourage experimentation and habituation—has much logical appeal and finds support in a wealth of anecdotal experiential evidence, but the body of formal research on the question, examined above, is not definitive.

Tombstone Advertising

Instead of banning advertising, policy could restrict its content. A common proposal in this area is that tobacco product advertising be restricted to "tombstone advertising," a mode in which no models, slogans, scenes, or colors are permitted. Tombstone ads could be restricted to pictures of the cigarette packages (with no models or scenery permitted on the packs) or to the brand name only, possibly restricted by type size, shape, and color, perhaps supplemented with prescribed data on tar, nicotine, and carbon monoxide, for example, and price.[80]

The Federal Trade Commission is charged with monitoring advertising for false or misleading claims. Tombstone advertising might be justified on the grounds that it is the only form of advertising that is not in violation of such standards. According to proponents of this approach, the advantage of restricting advertising to the tombstone mode is that the free-speech issue is mitigated, while the false and misleading imagery is avoided. Furthermore, by permitting data on tar, nicotine, CO, and price, tombstone ads would allow dissemination of factual and useful information to consumers, as the advertisers claim they want to provide.

The most obvious weakness of the tombstone approach is that it does not begin to address the growth area of cigarette promotion, its nonadvertising forms. A second possible disadvantage is that, to the extent that the manufacturers continued to advertise, the influence of ad revenues on publications' coverage of tobacco would remain. It must be assumed, however, that restriction of advertising to the tombstone mode would cause manufacturers to substantially reduce the volume of their advertising and correspondingly hasten the shift toward nonadvertising forms of promotion. Reduction in conventional advertising would mitigate the revenue-influence issue, if not eliminate it.

Enforcement of an Advertising and Promotion Code

Perhaps the least intrusive approach to restricting the false and misleading imagery of tobacco ads would be to develop a code defining permissible imagery in tobacco ads and then to develop an effective mechanism to assure that the Federal Trade Commission monitored advertising and strictly enforced compliance with the code. A good starting point for such a code might be the manufacturers' own voluntary advertising guidelines, developed in the 1960s.

In a similar context, the R.J. Reynolds "open debate" campaign could be interpreted for what it is: product promotion. In this capacity, all of the ads in the series could be required to bear the Surgeon General's health warning label. As a remedy to the misleading material the company has published, the Federal Trade Commission or the courts could require Reynolds to disclose in future ads that there is no genuine controversy on the hazards of tobacco.

The FTC's failure to respond expeditiously to the request to seek a remedy in the case of the ad entitled "Of Cigarettes and Science," combined with a history of lengthy FTC negotiations with tobacco advertisers on other advertising matters,[111] suggests the difficulty of establishing an effective procedure to assure compliance. Further, experience in Great Britain with agreements developed collaboratively by the government and the tobacco industry has not been encouraging in this regard.[116] The least restrictive of the alternatives we consider, the development of an advertising code also seems least likely to have any significant effect on the adverse impacts attributed to tobacco advertising. As in the case of tombstone advertising, it would not address other forms of promotion, although there, too, legal codes of acceptable behavior could be developed. For example, manufacturers could be forced to comply with their stated standards of not distributing product samples to children and not engaging in sampling activities near centers of youth activity.

Counteradvertising

Perhaps the most discussed alternative to a promotion ban is development of a means of funding a substantial counteradvertising campaign, a paid use of the media that could carry the tobacco-and-health message to the public with a frequency equal to at least a significant fraction of that achieved by tobacco advertisers. The concept of a media antitobacco campaign appeals to large segments of the public health community, primarily because experience with the Fairness Doctrine messages on TV and radio from 1967-70 was so successful. Empirical analysis has documented that the antis-moking messages, produced by the major voluntary health organizations and the federal government, depressed cigarette consumption much more than pro-smoking advertising encouraged it.[83] This accomplishment was particularly impressive in light of the much greater frequency of the latter and their greater concentration in prime time, as well as the amateurish quality of many of the antismoking messages.[91]

The major problem with the counteradvertising strategy is how to fund it. For a counteradvertising campaign to match even a tenth of the expenditures the tobacco industry devotes to promotion would require $200 million. A quarter of the industry effort would necessitate $500 million. These amounts substantially exceed the resources that could even conceivably be made available through the major voluntary agencies' combined budgets, not to mention the minimal sums devoted to the federal government's Office on Smoking and Health.

Two policies could raise the needed resources. One would be the development of a requirement that tobacco advertisers pay for an equivalent amount of space (or some fractional amount) to be used by organizations promoting understanding of the health consequences of smoking, such as the major voluntary associations and the Office on Smoking and Health. According to proponents of this approach, an "equal space" requirement would permit the public to receive some balance in its exposure to the characteristics of tobacco products.

While the notion of having tobacco advertisers pay for advertising space to combat their products may seem remarkable, the practice is already in effect: all cigarette ads are required to carry the Surgeon General's warning. The fact that the counteradvertising proposal seems so radical simply emphasizes how relatively ineffectual the Surgeon General's warning seems to be. The lesson of the warning is that a small written message cannot compete for attention with the much larger slick visual imagery of tobacco ads.[80] Large, visually slick counterads might compete successfully.

The second policy would be to earmark a few pennies of the federal cigarette excise tax to pay for a media antitobacco campaign. Each penny of the federal tax generates almost $300 million, so even as little as one penny devoted to the effort would permit a visible campaign. For the typical pack-and-a-half per day smoker, a one-cent tax would amount to less than $5.50 per year, while a five-cent earmarked tax—generating almost $1.5 billion—would cost the smoker just over $27 annually. The tax has the desirable feature of yielding diminishing revenue as consumption—and hence need for antitobacco publicity—falls. The earmarking proposal could also be applied at the level of state government. In recent years, a handful of states have begun to earmark cigarette taxes for a variety of health and health care purposes, but thus far no state has created substantial resources for a media antismoking campaign.

The idea of government purchasing advertising time might strike some observers as being inappropriate, or at least unusual. While appropriateness might be debated, the practice has considerable precedence. Currently, the federal government purchases ad time for the Departments of Defense and Transportation, and authority exists for the Department of Energy to buy time for energy conservation advertising.

These two options for funding a counteradvertising campaign have quite different implications in one important capacity: the first must be construed as an alternative to an advertising ban; it depends on the continued existence of tobacco advertising to materialize. In contrast, the second need not be considered an alternative. Drawing on tax revenues, the counteradvertising campaign could exist concurrently with a ban on tobacco promotion. The probable effects of the options might be dissimilar as well. If, for example, the "equal space" regulation required that the counteradvertising space be adjacent to that of the tobacco ad, it is likely that the regulation would dramatically decrease the amount of tobacco advertising, and thereby counteradvertising, and hasten the trend toward nonadvertising promotion of tobacco products.

Other Possibilities

Other approaches to addressing the perceived deleterious effects of tobacco promotion range from variations of the preceding regulatory themes to nonregulatory voluntary efforts. Illustrative of the former would be partial bans, perhaps prohibiting advertising and promotional activities to which substantial numbers of children might be exposed. For example, all ads on billboards and those in magazines with significant readerships under age 21 might be prohibited, along with a ban on sports and rock concert sponsorship and distribution of sample products on city streets. The attraction of a ban on ads and promotional activities reaching children is that the concept of "legal-to-buy, legal-to-advertise" is not violated, since underage children may not legally purchase cigarettes in most states. In a similar vein, in Great Britain a recent agreement between the government and the tobacco industry bans cigarette ads from movie theaters and more than two dozen women's magazines. Lasting for three years, the agreement also limits outdoor cigarette advertising to half of the 1980 level.[199]

Tax policy could represent an alternative regulatory approach. While the excise tax earmarking remains merely a concept, an alternative tax policy proposal is currently before Congress: ending the tax deductibility of tobacco advertising and promotion expenditures. The sponsors of this proposal, Senator Bradley and Representative Stark, argue that taxpayers should not subsidize the advertising of the nation's leading cause of premature death. The constitutionality of this proposal seems to be much less in doubt than the overall ban, as there is no constitutional "right" to tax deductions.

Most of the above proposals involve federal government action. In part, this emphasis reflects the obvious notion that the biggest impact could be achieved at this level. It also reflects an anomalous legal situation, however. One of the provisions of the federal Public Health Cigarette Smoking Act of 1969, referred to as the preemption clause, specifically prohibits the states from regulating cigarette advertising; the federally legislated restrictions "preempt" state action. Little noted at the time of the law's passage, the preemption clause has come to be recognized as a major asset for the cigarette manufacturers, since it is widely believed that individual states would have taken action on their own, had the law permitted them to do so, as it does regarding other products. In addition to creating a laboratory of potentially interesting experiments and innovations, the possibility of state-level regulation would greatly increase the difficulty of the tobacco industry's lobbying efforts to avoid restrictions on advertising and promotion. The perceived importance of the preemption clause is suggested by the American Lung Association's recently (May 1986) calling for its repeal.[200]

While attention in the tobacco advertising debate currently focuses on the public policy arena, and particularly that of the federal government, we should note in closing a review of "policy" options that the voluntary sector can mount nonmandated efforts that could also affect tobacco advertising and promotion. Illustrative would be consumer boycotts of publications accepting tobacco ads, or of a particular brand of heavily advertised cigarettes, or of sporting events sponsored by tobacco companies. Alternatively, a visible nontobacco product of a major tobacco conglomerate could be the object of a boycott, an idea proposed by APHA President William Foege.[201] A second nonregulatory voluntary effort could involve physicians cancelling subscriptions to tobacco-advertising magazines for their waiting rooms, making sure to inform the magazines of their reason for the cancellations and discussing the effort with the media. The American Lung Association recently issued a call for the removal of all magazine cigarette ads from doctors' waiting rooms.[200]

CHAPTER 7

SHOULD TOBACCO ADVERTISING AND PROMOTION BE BANNED?

The two essential facts that establish cigarette advertising and promotion as a topic of vital public health concern are the morbidity and mortality toll of cigarettes and the massive and multifaceted campaign to promote the product. Each of these facts represents an extreme: cigarettes are the leading cause of premature death and avoidable illness, and their advertising and promotion budget is the largest for any product. Neither of these extreme positions would be essential to mark cigarette promotion as a public policy concern, but together they do spotlight its importance on the stage of public health policy issues.

The nation's leading health officer has called smoking the most important public health issue of our time; he has called for a smoke-free society by the year 2000.[202] Yet the average American views the cigarette pandemic with ignorance of its importance and an associated complacency. This is readily understandable. The product is mundane and ever-present and its disease-causing mechanisms subtle, impossible to "see" or "feel". Smoking-related illness typically occurs in the middleaged and elderly, commonly decades after the habit was initiated; yet new recruits are children, imbued with a sense of immortality, to whom middle and old age are almost abstractions having little personal relevance. That these children will become the next generation of cigarettes' victims results from the addictiveness of smoking, a phenomenon that also has little meaning or personal relevance to a teenager or a pre-teen.

The pervasive glamorization of smoking—in magazine and newspaper ads, on billboards, in sporting events and concerts—perpetuates the association of smoking with maturity, sophistication, success, sex appeal, and athletic prowess—imagery certain to appeal to adolescents. Further, the very legality of cigarette advertising and promotion serves as an implicit endorsement of the belief that smoking "can't really be all that bad," a view to which many smokers and potential smokers want to subscribe. The legality contradicts and thereby diminishes official governmental pronouncements on the hazards of tobacco. Those pro-

97

nouncements, presented in the drab language of science and bureaucracy, are dwarfed in quantity and attractiveness by the pro-smoking message, which exemplifies the most appealing imagery that Madison Avenue has to offer.

In this context, the tug of war for the hearts and minds of potential smokers would appear to be no contest. Yet the imbalance is greater still, for the influence of the cigarette manufacturers greatly exceeds the attention they can buy directly with $2 billion in promotional expenditures: they also buy a measure of silence from the media. That measure has been enlarged recently by the two dominant firms' acquisitions of Nabisco and General Foods. In magazines that crusade on illicit drugs and environmental hazards, on overweight and stress, silence about tobacco only serves to reinforce the public's perception that smoking is simply one more risk among dozens, a risk factor less important than the absence of smoke detectors in the home. Yet cigarettes, alone, annually kill more Americans than do all of the following together: heroin, cocaine, alcohol, fire, automobiles, homicide, suicide, and AIDS.*

Should tobacco advertising and promotion be banned? The issues are numerous and often complex. While principle—most notably, the freedom of commercial speech—lies at the center of articulated opposition to a ban, pragmatic bottom-line concerns undoubtedly weigh heavily on the minds of the advertisers, media, and tobacco representatives who oppose a ban. A ban would hurt some publications; it might jeopardize selected athletic and cultural events; it would withdraw hundreds of millions of dollars from the nation's advertising agencies.

Would it reduce sales of tobacco products? The tobacco industry

---

* This is not intended to imply that smoking necessarily represents a greater health or social problem than these other sources of death and misery. Each has a unique set of consequences which are not strictly comparable. For example, while cocaine and heroin cause relatively few deaths, they are enormously destructive of the potential of their users and they create substantial fear and crime. While alcohol kills many fewer people than does tobacco, it is highly socially and emotionally disruptive and may well be more socially costly.[203] Similarly, motor vehicle accidents kill only a seventh or an eighth as many people as smoking, but the victims of the former are disproportionately teenagers and young adults, while the latter are predominantly middleaged and old. The comparison in the text simply presents a fact pertaining to the absolute number of premature deaths. In that context, the toll of smoking exceeds the sum of the other enumerated causes of death by 50 to 100 percent.

and its advertising association colleagues insist that it would not. Much logical evidence and some analytical evidence suggest the contrary, although not all. The tobacco industry's vocal opposition to a ban is itself testimony that the industry does not believe its own stated position: if advertising and promotion do not increase consumption, then their cessation would increase industry profits and might even increase consumption, by permitting reductions in the prices of tobacco products. If such were the case, the industry would support a ban. Their support of the 1971 broadcast ad ban demonstrated that they are more interested in the economic than the philosophical bottom line.

The fate of the nation's magazines and sports events is a legitimate concern, but it should not be exaggerated. Experience in this regard with the broadcast media following the broadcast ad ban proved much less dire than ban opponents had predicted. As important as tobacco advertising and promotion may be, they are not so dominant as to threaten the viability of entire institutions. A few economically marginal publications or sports events might be victims of an ad ban, but only a few. That this is of genuine concern, however, emphasizes how complacently we view the toll of tobacco, how accepting we are of the product. No one would express similar concern for the viability of a magazine if it were reliant on ad revenues for cocaine. But then, of course, cocaine is an illicit drug, while cigarettes are a legal product.

The legality of tobacco products is the foundation of opposition to the ban proposal. From it emanates the principle that truthful advertising of a legal product is a vital component of free speech, protected by the First Amendment. Espousal of this principle may be grounded in large part in immediate practical concerns— advertisers' fear of a significant loss of business, the media's fear of loss of substantial advertising revenues, tobacco companies' fear of loss of market—but there is also a genuine concern with erosion of commercial free speech liberties. Known as "the slippery slope," this concern sees the banning of tobacco advertising and promotion as opening the door to bans on the advertising of other hazardous products. The slippery slope argument, however, ignores the qualitative and quantitative uniqueness of tobacco. It is the only major legal product that is hazardous when used as intended, and its toll of premature death and avoidable illness exceeds that of every other consumer product. Further, the slippery slope never materialized following the broadcast ad ban.

Since the legality of tobacco products lies at the heart of opposition to a ban, the nature of this legality must be thoroughly appreciated. Tobacco products are legal solely by extraordinary exception, the result of historic accident. Tobacco became a widespread phenomenon, glamorized to the point of often being socially obligatory, well before the hazards of tobacco became known to medical science. The popularity of tobacco and its insidious addictiveness created a nation in which tens of millions of citizens were dependent users. They, in turn, served as role models for successive generations.

The existence of such a huge tobacco-dependent population makes the option of banning tobacco products wholly impractical and undesirable. The addictiveness of tobacco would turn millions of honest citizens into criminals, reliant on a black market that undoubtedly would come under the influence of organized crime; Prohibition taught this country a valuable lesson that has direct relevance in this case. Besides, there is a legitimate smoker's interest in the legal availability of tobacco products, effectively articulated by Michael Pertschuk, former chairman of the Federal Trade Commission:

There's a recognizable smoker's freedom at stake in this debate: a genuine, recognizable freedom: the freedom of consenting, mature adults, spared the psychological manipulation of Madison Avenue during adolescence, fully informed by a free and responsive media, to choose to smoke in the privacy of their homes. That's a freedom worthy of some respect. The rest is grotesque propaganda.[204]

It is important to emphasize that cigarettes would be illegal, or their use at least highly restricted, if they had not been singled out for exceptional treatment under the federal legal and regulatory apparatus applying to consumer products and the environment. If tobacco were treated like any other consumer product, its safety, output of products of combustion, and so on, would fall within the purview of a dozen or more federal agencies. Most noteworthy, perhaps, is the fact that the Consumer Products Safety Commission has been specifically precluded by federal law from considering the safety of cigarettes. Ironically, cigarettes cause damage enormously greater than that of the total of all the products the Commission has investigated.

With the legality of tobacco products dependent on such exceptional circumstances, the commercial free speech issue is mitigated. In addition, according to its recent decision, the Supreme Court finds little threat to First Amendment freedoms in the banning of even truthful advertising of products and services that are dangerous or sufficiently offensive to community standards of morality. The government, the Court noted, has the constitutional right to ban these products and services outright; thus the legality of banning advertising for them—a less restrictive step—seems only logical.

Despite all of this, the burden of proof in the current debate on the ad ban clearly rests on proponents of the ban, and on their advocating deviation from a status quo with firmly entrenched economic interests. This is reflected in the emphasis placed by both sides on determining whether advertising and promotion increase consumption, and particularly whether they entice children to initiate tobacco habits. One can imagine other circumstances in which the fundamental issues would be the consequences of the product and the character of efforts to encourage its use. In such a debate, emphasis would shift to the ethics of promoting the leading cause of premature death, and the burden of proof would shift to the opponents of a ban.

At the end, we return to two basic questions: should tobacco advertising and promotion be banned? Will they be? Given the complex workings of the U.S. Congress, the second question cannot be answered. Congress seems likely to struggle with the issue for months or even years. In their time-honored tradition, the lawmakers will contemplate alternatives and compromises, including those described in the preceding chapter. One of these seems worthy of the health community's consideration: a counteradvertising campaign with resources guaranteed to at least equal a sizable fraction (e.g., a fourth) of those devoted to tobacco advertising and promotion. Beyond it, however, it is difficult to imagine an alternative or a compromise that can address the varied concerns of the health community and have much prospect of significant impact.

Would a comprehensive ban have a substantial impact on the use of tobacco products? The evidence we have surveyed does not reveal an absolutely conclusive answer. Ultimately, however, the need for a definitive assessment may prove as unnecessary as it is elusive. Certainty, or the search for it, is the life's blood of

101

the scholar; ambiguity, and probability, are both the dominant realities of life and the currency of politics and the law. If the causal relationship between advertising and consumption were the issue, a legal or legislative judgment would be expected to rest on presumption, rather than irrefutable proof. In its entirety, the evidence is sufficient to make a strong presumptive case that the causal relationship exists.

While pragmatic concerns may dominate the debate, ethical issues cannot be evaded. As noted above, one can question the ethics of permitting tobacco promotion on the grounds of the inherent impropriety of promoting the leading cause of premature death. Beyond this, however, is a second ethical argument, one that is also firmly grounded in pragmatic public health: absent the elimination of tobacco products themselves, which is both impractical and undesirable, society has an obligation to its members to create an environment supportive of smokers' desire to quit and free of seductive enticements to children to start. The glamorous world of tobacco advertising, the temptation of the free sample, the intimidation of the media—these are antithetical to such an environment. A ban on tobacco promotion is an essential step toward creating that environment.

REFERENCES

1. US Department of Health and Human Services, Public Health Service: The Health Consequences of Smoking - Chronic Obstructive Lung Disease: A Report of The Surgeon General. DHHS Pub. No. (PHS) 84-50205. Washington, DC: Govt. Printing Office, 1984.
2. Rice DP, Hodgson TA: The economic costs of smoking, 1984. Unpublished manuscript. San Francisco, CA: University of California, 1986.
3. US Department of Health, Education, and Welfare, Public Health Service: Smoking and Health: A Report of the Surgeon General. DHEW Pub. No. (PHS) 79-50066. Washington, DC: Govt. Printing Office, 1979.
4. Ravenholt RT: Tobacco's impact on twentieth-century U.S. mortality patterns. Am J Prev Med 1985; 1:4-17.
5. Federal Trade Commission: Report to Congress, Pursuant to the Federal Cigarette Labeling and Advertising Act, for the Years 1982-1983. Washington, DC: FTC, June 1985, as revised December 1985.
6. Connolly GN, Winn DM, Hecht SS, et al: The reemergence of smokeless tobacco. New Engl J Med 1986; 314:1020-1027.
7. Johnston LD, O'Malley PN, Bachman JG: Drugs and American High School Students, 1975-83. Rockville, MD: National Institute on Drug Abuse, 1984.
8. US Department of Health and Human Services, Public Health Service: The Health Consequences of Using Smokeless Tobacco: A Report of the Advisory Committee to the Surgeon General. NIH Publication No. 86-2874. Washington, DC: Gov't Printing Office, 1986.
9. Marty PJ, McDermott RJ, Williams T: Patterns of smokeless tobacco use in a population of high school students. Am J Public Health 1986; 76:190-192.
10. Blum A: Selling cigarettes: the blue-collar black target. Washington Post, May 18, 1986, pp. F1, F4.
11. Remington PL, Forman MR, Gentry EM, et al: Current smoking trends in the United States: the 1981-1983 behavioral risk factor surveys. JAMA 1985; 253:2975-2978.
12. Buechner JS, Perry DK, Scott HD, et al: Cigarette smoking behavior among Rhode Island physicians. Am J Public Health 1986; 76:285-286.
13. US Department of Health and Human Services, Public Health Service: The Health Consequences of Smoking - Cancer and Chronic Lung Disease in the Workplace - A Report of the Surgeon General. DHHS (PHS) 85-50207. Washington, DC: Gov't Printing Office, 1985.
14. Working Party on the Effects of Passive Smoking on Health: Effects of Passive Smoking on Health. Australia: National Health and Medical Research Council, June 1986.
15. Smoking or Health: It's Your Choice. A Report by the American Council on Science and Health. Summit, NJ: ACSH, July 1984.
16. Decaisne G: The effects of tobacco smoking in children. JAMA 1883; 1:24-25.
17. Whelan EM: A Smoking Gun: How the Tobacco Industry Gets Away with Murder. Philadelphia, PA: George F. Stickley Co, 1984.
18. Wynder EL, Graham EA: Tobacco smoking as a possible etiologic factor in

bronchiogenic carcinoma: a study of 684 proved cases. JAMA 1950; 143:329-336.

19. Doll R, Hill AB: A study of the aetiology of carcinoma of the lung. Br Med J 1952; 2:1271-1286.

20. Doll R, Hill AB: The mortality of doctors in relation to their smoking habits: a preliminary report. Br Med J 1954; 1:1451-1455.

21. Office of Technology Assessment, U.S. Congress: Smoking-Related Deaths and Financial Costs. Washington, DC: OTA Staff Memorandum, September 1985.

22. US Department of Health and Human Services, Public Health Service: The Health Consequences of Smoking - Cancer: A Report of the Surgeon General. DHHS Pub. No. (PHS) 82-50179. Washington, DC: Govt. Printing Office, 1982.

23. Cancer Facts & Figures, 1985. New York, NY: American Cancer Society, 1985.

24. 1985 Annual Cancer Statistics Review. Washington, DC: National Cancer Institute, December 2, 1985.

25. Bailar JC, Smith EM: Progress against cancer? New Engl J Med 1986; 314:1226-1232.

26. US Department of Health and Human Services, Public Health Service: The Health Consequences of Smoking - Cardiovascular Disease: A Report of the Surgeon General. DHHS Pub. No. (PHS) 84-50204. Washington, DC: Govt. Printing Office, 1983.

27. Kuller LH, Meilahn E: Cigarette smoking - the primary cause of the epidemic of coronary heart disease deaths. Presented at the American Heart Association's 58th scientific sessions, Washington, DC, November 13, 1985.

28. Henningfield JE: Pharmacologic basis and treatment of cigarette smoking. Clinical Psychiatry 1984; 45:24-34.

29. Nicotine Dependency and Compulsive Tobacco Use. Boston, MA: Center for Health Communication, Harvard School of Public Health, June 19, 1986.

30. US Department of Health and Human Services, Public Health Service: Why People Smoke Cigarettes. PHS Pub. No. (PHS) 83-50195. Washington, DC: Govt. Printing Office, 1983.

31. American Psychiatric Association: Diagnostic and Statistical Manual of Mental Disorders, 3rd ed. Washington, DC: APA, 1980.

32. Kaplan J: The Hardest Drug: Heroin and Public Policy. Chicago, IL: University of Chicago Press, 1983.

33. Research shows that cigarette, heroin cravings similar. San Antonio Light, November 10, 1984, p. 88.

34. Greenberg RA, Haley NJ, Etsel RA, et al: Measuring the exposure of infants to tobacco smoke: nicotine and cotinine in urine and saliva. New Engl J Med 1984; 310:1075-1078.

35. Matsukura S, Taminato T, Kitano N, et al: Effects of environmental tobacco smoke on urinary cotinine excretion in nonsmokers: evidence for passive smoking. New Engl J Med 1984; 311;828-832.

36. White JR, Froeb HF: Small airway dysfunction in non-smokers chronically exposed to tobacco smoke. New Engl J Med 1980; 302:720-723.

37. Glantz SA, Jensen L: Bibliography on Involuntary Smoking. San Francisco, CA: University of California, March 1986.

38. Hirayama T: Non-smoking wives of heavy smokers have a higher risk of lung cancer: a study from Japan. Br Med J 1981; 282:183-185.

39. Here's what's now being said about tobacco smoke in the air. Wall Street J, August 10, 1981, p. 11.

40. Garfinkel L: Time trends in lung cancer mortality among non-smokers and a note on passive smoking. J Natl Cancer Inst 1981; 66:1061-1066.

41. Kuller LH, Garfinkel L, Correa P, et al: Passive Smoking and Lung Cancer. Workshop on the Contribution of Airborne Pullutants to Respiratory Cancer. Snowbird, UT, July 16-19, 1985.

42. Repace JL, Lowrey AH: A quantitative estimate of nonsmokers' lung cancer risk from passive smoking. Environ Int 1985; 11:3-22.

43. US Department of Health and Human Services, Public Health Service: The Health Consequences of Smoking for Women: A Report of the Surgeon General. Washington, DC: Govt. Printing Office, 1980.

44. Nieburg P, Marks JS, McLaren NM, et al: The fetal tobacco syndrome. JAMA 1985; 253:2998-2999.

45. Baird DD, Wilcox AJ: Cigarette smoking associated with delayed conception. JAMA 1985; 253:2979-2983.

46. Sperling D: Smoking, infertility tied. USA Today, October 16, 1985.

47. Bonham GS, Wilson RW: Children's health and families with cigarette smokers. Am J Public Health 1981; 71:290-293.

48. Tager IB, Weiss ST, Munoz A, et al: Longitudinal study of the effects of maternal smoking on pulmonary function in children. New Engl J Med 1983; 309:699-703.

49. McGuire A: Cigarettes and fire deaths. NY State J Med 1983; 83:1296-1298.

50. Miller LM, Monahan J: Wanted, and available, filter-tips that really filter. Reader's Digest, August 1957; 36:43-49.

51. Slade J, Tye JB: Asbestos in cigarettes. Unpublished manuscript. New Brunswick, NJ: Rutgers Medical School, 1986.

52. US Department of Health and Human Services, Public Health Service: The Health Consequences of Smoking - The Changing Cigarette: A Report of the Surgeon General. DHHS Pub. No. (PHS) 81-50156. Washington, DC: Govt. Printing Office, 1981.

53. Harris JE: Public policy issues in the promotion of less hazardous cigarettes. In: Gori GB, Bock FG (eds.): Banbury Report 3: A Safe Cigarette? Cold Spring Harbor, NY: Banbury Center, 1980, pp. 333-340.

54. Kozlowski LT, Frecker RC, Khouw V, et al: The misuse of less-hazardous cigarettes and its detection: hole blocking of ventilated filters. Am J Public Health 1980; 70:1202-1203.

55. Schachter S, Silverstein B, Kozlowski LT et al: Studies of the interaction of psychological and pharmacological determinants of smoking. J Experimental Psych 1977; 106:3-40.

56. Russell MAH, Jarvis M, Duer R, et al: Relation of nicotine yield of cigarettes to blood nicotine concentrations in smokers. Br Med J 1980; 280:972-6.

57. Kozlowski LT, Frecker RC, Lei H: Nicotine yields of cigarettes, plasma nicotine in smokers and public health. Prev Med 1982; 11:240-244.

58. Benowitz NL, Hall SM, Herning RI, *et al*: Smokers of low-yield cigarettes do not consume less nicotine. N Engl J Med 1983; 309:139-142.

59. Folsum AR, Pechacek TF, de Gaudemaris R, *et al*: Consumption of 'low yield' cigarettes: its frequency and relationship to serum thiocyanate. Am J Public Health 1984; 74:564-568.

60. Eysenck HJ: The Causes and Effects of Smoking. Beverly Hills, CA: Sage Publications, 1980.

61. Tobacco Institute: Cigarette Smoking and Cancer: A Scientific Perspective. Washington, DC: The Tobacco Institute, 1982.

62. Tollison RD: Smoking and Society: Toward a More Balanced Assessment. Lexington, MA: D.C. Heath, 1986.

63. Breslow L: Cigarette smoking and health. Public Health Rep 1980; 95:451-455.

64. Of cigarettes and science. Washington Post, March 19, 1985, p. A20.

65. Pear R: Reynolds faces F.T.C. charges in smoking ads; misrepresentation seen on hazards to health. NY Times, June 17, 1986, pp. 1, 11.

66. Second-hand smoke: the myth and the reality. The Philadelphia Inquirer Magazine, September 30, 1984, p. 11.

67. Cancer society aide's words with tobacco concerns twist. NY Times, June 5, 1984, p. A26.

68. Garfinkel L, Auerbach O, Joubert L: Involuntary smoking and lung cancer: a case-control study. JNCI 1985; 75:463-469.

69. Tye JB: A pack of lies: health claims in cigarette ads. Unpublished manuscript. Palo Alto, CA: Stop Teenage Addiction to Tobacco, June 1986.

70. Hahn PM, Cullman JF, Royster FS, *et al*: A frank statement to cigarette smokers. n.d.

71. McKenzie R: A loyalist views tobacco's fate. Insight, May 19, 1986, p. 15.

72. Norr R: Cancer by the carton. Reader's Digest, December 1952; 61:7-8.

73. Lieb C: Can the poisons in cigarettes be avoided? Reader's Digest, December 1953; 63:45-47.

74. Miller LM, Monahan J: The facts behind the cigarette controversy. Reader's Digest, July 1954; 65:1-6.

75. US Department of Health, Education, and Welfare, Public Health Service: Smoking and Health: Report of the Advisory Committee to the Surgeon General of the Public Health Service. DHEW Pub. No. (PHS) 1103. Washington, DC: Govt. Printing Office, 1964.

76. Warner KE: The effects of the anti-smoking campaign on cigarette consumption. Am J Public Health 1977; 67:645-650.

77. Gori GB, Lynch CJ: Toward less hazardous cigarettes. JAMA 1978; 240:1255-1257.

78. Homburger F: Socially tolerable cigarette smoke? JAMA 1979; 241:2142.

79. Warner KE: Toward less hazardous cigarettes. JAMA 1979; 241:2143.

80. Meyers ML, Iscoe C, Jennings C, *et al*: Staff Report on The Cigarette Advertising Investigation. Washington, DC: Federal Trade Commission, May 1981.

81. Warner KE: State legislation on smoking and health: a comparison of two policies. Policy Sciences 1981; 13:139-152.

82. Warner KE: Clearing the airwaves: the cigarette ad ban revisited. Policy Analysis 1979; 5:435-450.
83. Hamilton JL: The demand for cigarettes: advertising, the health scare, and the cigarette advertising ban. Rev Econ Stat 1972; 54:401-411.
84. Warner KE: Possible increases in the underreporting of cigarette consumption. J Amer Stat Assoc 1978; 73:314-318.
85. Where There's Smoke: Problems and Policies Concerning Smoking in The Workplace. Rockville, MD: Bureau of National Affairs, 1986.
86. Martin MJ, Silverman MF: The San Francisco experience with regulation of smoking in the workplace: the first twelve months. Am J Public Health 1986; 76:585-586.
87. Warner KE: Cigarette Smoking in the 1970's: the impact of the antismoking campaign. Science 1981; 211:729-731.
88. Warner KE: Smoking and health implications of a change in the federal cigarette excise tax. JAMA 1986; 255:1028-1032.
89. Lewit EM, Coate D: The potential for using excise taxes to reduce smoking. J Health Econ 1982; 1:121-146.
90. Lewit EM, Coate D, Grossman M: The effects of government regulation on teenage smoking. J Law Econ 1981; 24:545-569.
91. Green P: The mass media anti-smoking campaign around the world. In: US Department of Health, Education, and Welfare, National Institutes of Health: Proceedings/3rd World Conference on Smoking and Health, 1975.
92. Russell MA, Wilson C, Taylor C, et al: Effect of general practitioners' advice against smoking. Br Med J 1979; 2:231-235.
93. Wolinsky H: Burning issue: why did AMA kill smoking story? Seattle Times, March 25, 1984, p. A24.
94. Lundberg GD: Particularly sensitive political issues. Memo to editorial staff of JAMA, September 7, 1982.
95. DeLay WR: Letter to KE Warner, April 16, 1985.
96. Iglehart JK: Smoking and public policy. N Engl J Med 1984; 310:539-544.
97. JAMA 1984; 252:2789-2924.
98. JAMA 1985; 253:2925-3036.
99. JAMA 1986; 255:985-1084.
100. The World Cigarette Pandemic NY State J Med 1983; 83(13).
101. The World Cigarette Pandemic, Part II. NY State J Med 1985; 85(7).
102. Connell D, Turner R, Mason J, et al: Summary of findings of the school education evaluation: health promotion effectiveness, implementation, and cost. J School Health 1985; 55:316-321.
103. Gaps found in Americans' knowledge of health habits. Nation's Health, July 1986, p. 1.
104. The Prevention Index: A Report Card on the Nation's Health, Summary Report. Emmaus, PA: Rodale Press, 1984.
105. Marsh A, Matheson J: Smoking attitudes and behavior. An enquiry carried out on behalf of the Department of Health and Social Security, Office of Population Census and Surveys. London, England: HMSO, 1983.
106. Grise VN: Tobacco - Background for 1985 Farm Legislation. Washington, DC: US Department of Agriculture, Economic Research Service, Agriculture Information Bull. No. 468, September 1984.

107. US Department of Health, Education, and Welfare, Public Health Service: Use of Tobacco: Practices, Attitudes, Knowledge, and Beliefs, United States-Fall 1964 and Spring 1966. Washington, DC: Govt. Printing Office, 1969.

108. US Department of Health, Education, and Welfare, Public Health Service: Adult Use of Tobacco-1970. Atlanta, GA: Center for Disease Control, June 1973.

109. US Department of Health, Education, and Welfare, Public Health Service: Adult Use of Tobacco-1975. Atlanta, GA: Center for Disease Control, June 1976.

110. Survey of Attitudes Towards Smoking. Gallup Poll sponsored by American Lung Association, July 1985.

111. Calfee JE: Cigarette advertising, health information and regulation before 1970. Working paper. Washington, DC: Bureau of Economics, Federal Trade Commission, December 1985.

112. Ernster VL: Tobacco advertising over the years: types, themes, voluntary codes, and related legislation. Presented at the meeting of the Interagency Advisory Committee on Smoking and Health, Washington, DC, February 12, 1986.

113. Magnus P: Tobacco and the media. Unpublished manuscript, December 1983.

114. Tye JB: Sixty Years of Deception: An Analysis and Compilation of Cigarette Ads in Time Magazine, 1925 to 1985. Palo Alto, CA: Health Advocacy Center, 1986.

115. Friedman KM: Public Policy and the Smoking-Health Controversy. Lexington, MA: D.C. Heath, 1975.

116. Taylor P: The Smoke Ring: Tobacco, Money and Multinational Politics. New York, NY: Pantheon Books, 1984.

117. 'Promotions' to overtake cigarette 'advertising.' Smoking and Health Reporter 1986; 3(4):6.

118. Englander TJ: Cigarette makers shift ad strategies. United States Tobacco and Candy Journal 1986; 213(21):1, 46.

119. Warner KE: Tobacco industry response to public health concern: a content analysis of cigarette ads. Health Ed Q 1985; 12:115-127.

120. Okie S: Ad dollars seen inhibiting antismoking news: magazines appear to avoid antagonizing tobacco industry. Washington Post, December 11, 1985, pp. A1, A18.

121. 100 Leading National Advertisers. Advertising Age, September 14, 1984, pp. 28, 44, 132.

122. Garn SM: Smoking and human biology. Human Biology 1985; 57:505-523.

123. National Association of State Boards of Education: Helping Youth Decide. Alexandria, VA: NASBE, July 1984.

124. Whelan EM: Letter to H Kornegay, Chairman, Tobacco Institute. December 19, 1984.

125. Magnus P: Superman and the Marlboro woman. NY State J Med 1985; 85:342-343.

126. We're the tobacco industry too. The New Republic, October 1984, p. 21.

127. Beck J: Would you die to save a tobacco worker's job? Detroit Free Press, November 19, 1984, p. 9A.

128. Silver GA: Smoking: the union label. Washington Post, January 13, 1985, p. B7.

129. Warner KE: Tobacco Institute's new study of the economic impact of the tobacco industry. Memo to Interested Parties. Ann Arbor, MI: University of Michigan, March 11, 1986.

130. Hall T: Philip Morris, seeking to turn tide, attacks cigarette opponents. Wall Street J, February 14, 1986, pp. 1, 17.

131. Hall T: Philip Morris Co. magazine promotes pro-smoking issues. Wall Street J, July 24, 1985.

132. Goodman E: The most addictive drug. Washington Post, December 12, 1985.

133. Can television be replaced? Tobacco Reporter, August 1980, pp. 21-25.

134. Foote E: Advertising and tobacco. JAMA 1981; 245:1667-1668.

135. Ernster VL: Mixed messages for women: a social history of cigarette smoking and advertising. NY State J Med 1985; 85:335-340.

136. What have we learned from people? A conceptual summarization of 18 focus group interviews on the subject of smoking. Federal Trade Commission Staff Report on the Cigarette Advertising Investigation, Document A901268. Washington, DC: FTC, May 1975.

137. Chandler WU: Banishing Tobacco. Worldwatch paper 68. Washington, DC: Worldwatch Institute, 1986.

138. Wickstrom B: Cigarette Marketing in the Third World. Goteborg, Sweden: University of Gothenburg, 1979.

139. Ryan WP: Cigarette advertising - its role and rationale. Paper presented to Health Advisory Council, Health Commission of New South Wales, July 17, 1978.

140. Pertschuk, M: Statement of FTC Endorsement of Rotational Health Warnings Legislation and Additional Cigarette Advertising Issues. Washington, DC: Federal Trade Commission, May 3, 1984.

141. Hutchings R: A review of the nature and extent of cigarette advertising in the United States. National Conference on Smoking or Health - Developing a Blueprint for Action. New York, NY: American Cancer Society, 1981, pp. 249-262.

142. Waterson MJ: Advertising and cigarette consumption. *In:* Smoking Prevention Education Act, Hearings Before the Subcommittee on Health and the Environment, Committee on Energy and Commerce, U.S. House of Representatives, 98th Congress. 1st session - on H.R. 1824, March 9 and 17, 1983.

143. Lochsen PM, Bjartveit K, Hauknes A, *et al:* Trends in tobacco consumption and smoking habits in Norway. Report of the Norwegian Council on Smoking and Health. Presented at the Fifth World Conference on Smoking and Health, Winnipeg, Canada, July 1983.

144. Chapman S: Cigarette Advertising & Smoking: A Review of the Evidence. London, England: British Medical Association, March 1985.

145. Davis R: Proposed ban on tobacco-product advertising and promotion.

Unpublished paper. Chicago, IL: American Medical Association, January 1986.

146. Goldstein AO, Fischer PM, Richards JW, *et al*: The influence of cigarette advertising on adolescent smoking. Unpublished manuscript. Augusta, GA: Medical College of Georgia, 1986.

147. McCarthy WJ: Testimony presented at the Oversight Hearing on Tobacco Advertising and Promotion. Subcommittee on Health and the Environment, Committee on Energy and Commerce, U.S. House of Representatives, Washington, DC, July 18, 1986.

148. Bergler R: Advertising and Cigarette Smoking. Bern, Switzerland: Hans Huber, 1981.

149. Johnson LW: Advertising expenditure and aggregate demand for cigarettes in Australia. Unpublished manuscript. North Ryde, Australia: Macquarie University, June 1985.

150. Lambin JJ: Advertising, Competition and Market Conduct in Oligopoly Over Time. Amsterdam, Holland: North-Holland Publishing Co., 1976.

151. Metra Consulting Group: The Relationship Between Total Cigarette Advertising and Total Cigarette Consumption in the UK, 1979.

152. Schmalensee R: The Economics of Advertising. Amsterdam, Holland: North-Holland Publishing Co., 1972.

153. McGuiness T, Cowling K: Advertising and the aggregate demand for cigarettes. European Econ Rev 1975; 6:311-328.

154. Radfar M: The effect of advertising on total consumption of cigarettes in the UK. European Econ Rev 1985; 29:225-233.

155. Reuijl JC: On the Determination of Advertising Effectiveness - An Empirical Study of the German Cigarette Market. The Netherlands: Kluwer-Nijhoff Publishing, 1982.

156. Simon JL: The health economics of cigarette consumption. J Human Resources 1968; 3:111-117.

157. Telser LG: Advertising and cigarettes. J Political Economy 1962; 70:471-499.

158. Cox HT: Smoking, tobacco promotion, and the voluntary agreements. Br Med J 1984; 288:303-305.

159. Schneider L, Klein B, Murphy KM: Governmental regulation of cigarette health information. J Law Econ 1981; 24:575-612.

160. Hamilton JL: The effect of cigarette advertising bans on cigarette consumption. Proceedings of the 3rd World Conference on Smoking and Health, 1985, pp. 829-840.

161. Cummins K: The cigarette makers: how they get away with murder. Washington Monthly, April 1984, pp. 14-24.

162. Owen D: The cigarette companies: how they get away with murder. Part II. Washington Monthly, March 1985, pp. 48-54.

163. Owen D: A final word on the New Republic and those cigarette ads. Washington Monthly, June 1985, pp. 51-52.

164. Warner KE: Cigarette advertising and media coverage of smoking and health. New Engl J Med 1985; 312:384-388.

165. Whelan EM: When Newsweek and Time filtered cigarette copy. Wall Street J, November 1, 1984.

166. Seldes G: Lords of The Press. New York, NY: Julian Messner, 1938.
167. Bagdikian BH: The Media Monopoly. Boston, MA: Beacon Press, 1983.
168. Smith RC: The magazines' smoking habit. Columbia Journalism Rev 1978; 16(5):29-31.
169. Dale KC: ACSH survey: which magazines report the hazards of smoking? ACSH News and Views 1982; 3(3):1, 8-10.
170. Jacobson B, Amos A: When Smoke Gets In Your Eyes: Cigarette Advertising Policy and Coverage of Smoking and Health in Women's Magazines. London, England: British Medical Association, May 1985.
171. Whelan EM, Sheridan MJ, Meister KA, *et al:* Analysis of coverage of tobacco hazards in women's magazines. J Public Health Policy 1981; 2:28-35.
172. White L, Whelan EM: How well do American magazines cover the health hazards of smoking? The 1986 survey. ACSH News and Views 1986; 7(3):1, 8-11.
173. Warner KE: Tobacco ads choke off coverage of smoking peril. 1985-86 Journalism Ethics Report, Society of Professional Journalists, 1985, p. 27.
174. ABC News: Growing up in smoke. 20/20, Transcript of show no. 338, October 20, 1983.
175. Connolly GN: Testimony presented at the Oversight Hearing on Tobacco Advertising and Promotion. Subcommittee on Health and the Environment, Committee on Energy and the Environment, U.S. House of Representatives, July 18, 1986.
176. Guyon J: Do publications avoid anti-cigarette stories to protect ad dollars? Wall Street J, November 22, 1982, pp. 1, 22.
177. Gerard G: Letter to KE Warner, November 30, 1984.
178. Cirino R: Don't Blame the People. Los Angeles, CA: Diversity Press, 1971.
179. Emery CE, Jr: Tobacco industry's ad clout sounds an alarm. Providence J-Bull, April 23, 1986, pp. A1-A2.
180. Reinbold GA: Letter to KE Warner, March 2, 1984.
181. Pertschuk M: Letter to KE Warner, May 1986.
182. Gitlitz G: Cigarette advertising and The New York Times: an ethical issue that's unfit to print? NY State J Med 1983; 83:1284-1291.
183. Gitlitz GF: Drop cigarette advertising. New York Times, May 11, 1985.
184. McMillan HD: Letter to KE Warner, November 17, 1983.
185. Sammons JH: Letter to KE Warner, n.d.
186. Stacey J: Letter to G Weis, December 7, 1983.
187. McGinnis RD: Letter to The Editor, Time magazine (unpublished), October 17, 1984.
188. Whelan E: Smoking out the culprit. ACSH News and Views 1984; 5(1):4.
189. Warner KE, Murt HA: Premature deaths avoided by the antismoking campaign. Am J Public Health 1983; 73:672-677.
190. Roemer R: National legislative strategies to control cigarette advertising, promotion and marketing. Submitted to the Interagency Advisory Committee on Smoking and Health, Washington, DC, February 1, 1986.
191. Cancer unit urges all cigarette ads in nation be ended. NY Times, October 19, 1967, p. 94.
192. McDermott S: Letter to KE Warner, June 16, 1986.

193. Blasi V, Monaghan HP: Letter to KB Johnson, General Counsel, American Medical Association, March 18, 1986.

194. Killian JH: Congressional research service says ad ban constitutional. ASH Smoking and Health Rev 1986; 16:4-13.

195. White L: A total ban on cigarette advertising: is it constitutional? ACSH News and Views 1984; 5(4):1, 4-7.

196. Miller M: The first amendment and legislative bans of liquor and cigarette advertisements. Columbia Law Rev 1985; 85:632-655.

197. Neuborn B: The wrong way to stop smoking. Washington Post, July 18, 1986.

198. Taylor S: High court, 5-4, sharply limits constitutional protection for ads. New York Times, July 2, 1986, pp. 1, 34.

199. British cigarette ad restrictions. Smoking and Health Rep 1986; 3(4):6.

200. Bailey WJ: A.L.A. calls for ban on cigarette ads in doctors' waiting rooms and asks for removal of federal preemption clause. Smoking and Health Reporter 1986; 3(4):1,4.

201. Foege calls for a boycott of a tobacco company's other products. The Nation's Health, May-June 1985, p. 3.

202. Koop CE: A smoke-free society by the year 2000. Julia M Jones lecture presented to the annual meeting of the American Lung Association, Miami Beach, FL, May 20, 1984.

203. Luce BR, Schweitzer SO: Smoking and alcohol abuse: a comparison of their economic consequences. N Engl J Med 1978; 298:569-571.

204. Pertschuk M: Strategy and tactics. Presented at the Conference on Smoking and Reproductive Health, San Francisco, CA, October 14, 1985.